Telling Stories Like Jesus Did

CHRISTELLE L. ESTRADA

Resource Publications, Inc.
160 East Virginia Street, Suite 290
San Jose, California 95112

Editorial director: Kenneth Guentert
Production editor: Elizabeth J. Asborno
Cover design: Ron Niewald
Cover illustration: Nancy LaBerge Muren
Production assistant: Allison Cunningham

ISBN 0-89390-097-4

Library of Congress Card Catalog Number 86-62626

6 5 4 3 2 | 93 92 91 90 89

Resource Publications, Inc.
160 E. Virginia Street, Suite 290
San Jose, CA 951112-5848

Some of these stories originally appeared in Catechist *magazine.*

In Gratitude:

To my family and those who have touched my life deeply.

They are forever STORY for me.

CONTENTS

Acknowledgments vii
Preface ix
Introduction 1

I. The Invitation (Luke 19:1-10) 9
II. The Forgiving Parents (Luke 15:11-32) 17
III. The Gift (Luke 21:1-4) 25
IV. The Guests (Luke 10:38-41) 33
V. The Lost Kitten (Luke 15:1-10) 39
VI. The Loving Neighbor (Luke 10:25-37) 47
VII. The Party (Luke 18:9-14;14:7-11) 55
VIII. The One Thank You (Luke 17:11-19) 63
IX. The Sorry Story (Luke 7:36-47) 69
X. The Busy Teacher (Luke 18:1-8) 77
XI. An Anywhere, Anytime Parable 85

Resources 93

ACKNOWLEDGMENTS

I especially acknowledge the encouragement I received from the faculty and staff at Holy Name of Jesus School in South Central Los Angeles. I am indebted to the students of Holy Name who played out these stories in classroom sessions and liturgical celebrations. In particular, I am grateful for the second-grade students; their enthusiasm for the stories in this book proved to be the motivation I needed when I thought I could not do one more revision or write one more line. The memories we share are precious to me.

I would like to thank the people of Shiprock and Crownpoint, New Mexico, who shared so generously their lives and stories with me; in the sharing, they encouraged me to live out the faithfulness and Truth of my personal life journey.

Lastly, I acknowledge the interest and support of those at the School of Theology at Claremont, especially those Process Theologians and Constructivists who are forever looking for creative ways to integrate theory and practice across many disciplines.

PREFACE

Stories, like books, grow and have a life of their own. They emerge in specific contexts and, through their particularity, speak to the heart. When stories are shared, the listeners change and, in the hearing, so does each story. This has been my experience of the stories in this book.

These stories began as ad libs for a group of second graders in inner-city Los Angeles. For these children I changed the Lost Sheep to the Lost Kitten. The only sheep they had ever seen had been in books. When I told this story in Shiprock, New Mexico, to a group of Navajo children, I changed it back to the Lost Sheep. The obvious reason being that all of the children had a more intense experience with lambs than with kittens. Of course I asked them first about their experiences with sheep and kittens. This is the task of preparing students for story. By engaging students in naming their experience, you can use what they name to help create the riverbanks through which the story flows.

Over the course of two years, 1986-87, I worked on introductions and reflection questions. At the time, they included perspectives that I had found valuable in my own education ministry with children and teachers in the inner city. They emphasized ethical models and ways to act inclusively in a pluralistic society, a more community-centered approach.

As I have changed and grown on my life journey, I have become conscious of certain psychological dynamics in dependent and codependent relationships (see Anne Wilson Shaef in "Resources" section). Patterns of behavior that often are disguised as self-sacrifice become ways to control others. This behavior denies my own goodness and justifies self-hate by suspecting God's gifts to be conditioned.

Sometimes control manifests itself by clinging to truth as never-changing. This clinging provides a secure feeling based on an image of the world as static and of my identity separate from God's lifegiving spirit in the world. However, through God's grace embodied in me, I can awaken more fully to the life spirit within the entire biotic community. I feel the breath of life energy in trees, in animals, in rocks, in myself, and in others.

God's gift of life active in the world is, for the Christian, the gift of the Incarnation. For the contemplative person, it is the sacramentality of the present moment. For the Buddhist, it is Buddha nature or enlightened compassion. For the Judaist, it is the Genesis affirmation that creation is good. For indigenous peoples, it is the Great Spirit within the world. Every tradition is not the same, but in the diversity of many perspectives, the whole emerges.

My heightened awareness of the sacredness of the ordinary, my exposure to more diverse cultural contexts, and my involvement in interreligious dialogue have shifted my perspectives and altered my worldview. I call this shift a sensitivity to the aesthetic rhythms of life. This sensitivity does not set the community in opposition to the individual but affirms a person-centered approach to curriculum theory as a way to enrich the community. I image this approach as a tapestry instead of a melting pot or mosaic. Each individual thread, by manifesting its own diversity and magnificence, adds texture and colorful rhythm to the whole. The beauty of the individual is the beauty of the community. The beauty of an ethnic community is the beauty of the planetary community, which in turn creates subtle hues in the cosmic story.

In this context and with this image, I envision my role as a religious educator as having a twofold function. First, I need to create an environment in which the practical application of unconditional love affirms the individual diversity of each person and each culture. Second, I need to make sure that trust in individual integrity (whether a person or a culture) affirms the belief that God's grace is working in my and my student' lives in every moment and with every breath. Grace *is* the Creative Energy that makes life an adventure, even in the midst of difficulty and pain.

This understanding of aesthetic rhythms is based on my reclaiming the cultural gifts of my own ethnic heritage. This heritage is stored in the memory of the indigenous peoples of the Southwest and Mexico. I am grateful for these memories, and I express thankfulness to my four grandparents whose names and spirits are sung by the four winds. With them I say the Navajo prayer:

Hozhoongo naashaa doo. I walk in beauty.

INTRODUCTION

My best memories of childhood are times when I was deeply involved in the miracle of storytelling. Every night I asked my mother to read *The Adventures of Babar* to me. I knew the story by heart, yet Mother read it as if it were forever new. Like fabric woven with strands of voice, touch, and patience, these bedtime memories clothe me still with the warmth of what it means to be loved.

This is part of the magic of storytelling. The wonder of the story is not only the story itself, but the people who tell the story. My grandfather told me stories of Hiawatha through Longfellow's poetry. His recitation was accompanied by Indian whoops and hollers and little war dances. My father's stories were different. They came from his own life experiences with his family during the Depression. These sixty-second rememberings have significantly altered my perception of the world, family, and my place in the universe.

Reading and telling stories are powerful dimensions of life, but listening to stories has an energy of its own. My grandmother never told stories. She listened to mine and in the listening became the story herself. Every day after school I sat with Grandmother on her back porch and we ate grapefruit together. She would ask me to draw for her.

"What shall I draw for you today, Grandmother?" I always asked. She would pause and think.

"A train with a grandmother riding on top." The answer was always the same and so was the drawing. She knew that's what I could draw and her knowing made me happy.

These memories are palpable and rich. Their texture keeps me warm on cold, rainy days. They bring to my life a sense of eternity and myth because myth is the reality that creates the story. My grandparents are both dead, but their lives continue. They are story for me, story that feeds and nourishes like bread and wine.

My fondest memories of teaching are the times when I became part of the miracle of someone else's story. An eighth-grade girl gave me a Wrigley's gum wrapper chain on the last day of school. Shoving it into my hands she said, "This is my life," and ran away. Second-grade students answer questions with disjointed, seemingly unrelated stories from their everyday world. The words they use oftentimes do not say what they mean. Yet, it is this very ambiguity that allows the listener to participate in the storytelling.

Recent religion textbooks have used the storytelling technique quite well. Children's bibles have made exciting stories of the past come to life through colorful illustrations and easier language. Theologians have detailed the implications of Jesus as storyteller and have moved us more deeply into the person of Jesus. Yet, there seems to be another dimension in storytelling that is needed as well.

When Jesus spoke, he used current events and experiences surrounding his listeners. He used paradoxes to shock his listeners into action, choice, or divergent thought. For example, the child in Los Angeles listens to the story of the Good Samaritan. A city named Jericho is far removed from the child's experience. The Samaritan being a good neighbor is a shocker, if you are a Jew living in Palestine in the first century. If you are a child in an American city in the 1980s, maybe a bag lady as good neighbor is more of a surprise.

Good stories are miracles of wonder and power because they take us where we rarely go on our own. They take us into our own interior geography and help us chart new, exciting territory. Stories not only help us define ourselves, but also help us resonate with what is deepest in the experience of others.

The following stories have been used in various ways with a variety of age levels. They have helped catechists clothe the Gospel stories with the nowness of our own lives. It is a telling that helps each of us experience the story of Jesus all over again.

In this collection, with the exception of the "Anywhere, Anytime Parable," the stories are chosen from the Gospel of Luke. Each story describes how we can live the Good News of salvation. Looking at the word "salvation," in its original Latin meaning, we discover that it means health and wholeness. Salvation, therefore, is a way of living in the world that proclaims peace and Thanksgiving in the midst of difficulty. It is movement toward unity in a world broken by differences. In each story, the Christian vision is imaged as an ever-widening circle, spiralling outward to include differences while being enriched by them. This symbol has been significant in my own life and has provided a framework for the introductions in this anthology. For this insight and many others included in this work, I am indebted to the writings of Alfred North Whitehead.

The Gospel proclamation of inclusivity, health, happiness, and belonging is a fact that children can easily understand. They have the innate ability to enjoy life now because, unlike many adults, they understand that it's safe to know what they want. They know when they are happy and what makes them feel good. Children intuitively understand how to create a better world and celebrate God's presence in it. To them a better world is simple. It is experiencing life full of activity, novelty, and celebration.

This fullness of life is based on three interconnected themes that color and texture the experiences of children. The first theme can be called "eucharistic family." To celebrate a birthday meal at the local pizza parlor or share junk-food snacks on the playground, personifies the need to be with friends, meet new people, and party. This ritual action of children symbolically embodies the paradigm of table-fellowship. To sit down and share a meal or apple with thanksgiving in a non-judgmental way is to open the doors to eucharistic family in every moment of life.

The second theme is feeling the "welcoming home" of family after things have gone wrong. This "home-sense"is the basic impulse toward integration, healing, and reconciliation. As adults, we often numb this desire for re-integration into community and replace it with a kind of rugged individualism that isolates us from the richness of interdependence. To feel the "home-sense" of children is to weave the strands of our lives into a magical, cosmic fabric whose intertwining makes us both free for being who we really are and truly whole because of our interconnections with all reality.

The third theme that children intuitively bring to life is self-acceptance. Children accept themselves and desire to accept others. This quality of childlike acceptance creates friendships in spite of differences that adults often see as insurmountable. Children understand intuitively that friendship is a connecting point. It spins their life into a rhythmic harmony with everything in their world. Being able to be absorbed in the flight of a butterfly or the life of an anthill is the kind of wonder children use to make friends with the universe.

How many times have we seen children bereft because their friends won't talk to them or share their toys? Yet, in one simple reconciling gesture of play, all is forgiven and, yes, forgotten. This childlike attitude is essential in developing an acceptance of unconditional love. In spite of what they have, who they know, where they live, children expect and trust the fact of unconditional love. As they grow older, suspicion of others and self-doubt block this belief. Unconditional love, then, is what the catechist//teacher is called to model. This love is the kind of love God is for each of us.

These three themes color the parables in this collection and emphasize the kind of Jesus-actions that show us not only who God is, and how we should live, but also who we really are. The power of each Gospel story transcends the culture of first century Palestine, when WE creatively incorporate our students' cultural, ethnic, and social experiences into stories about their world. It is through these concrete particularities that the universal emerges, shining sunlight on the ordinary events of everyday life. This is the power of the community's past experience of Jesus coming full force into our own lives in the present and luring us on to future possibilities. As a storyteller, Jesus used parables to show how patterns of behaving could be enlivened by something NEW. He called his listeners to a different way of thinking about traditions. This is the power of the future already present in the hearing of the Gospel story. Jesus challenged his listeners to decide about how they wanted to live. This is the power of the present, which, for Jesus, was always the moment of decision. Jesus was a great storyteller because his stories introduced his listeners to surprise, the unexpected. He creatively lured them to see a new possibility for living a happy, healthy life.

Each story, before being experienced, should first be read from the Gospel by the teacher/catechist. Reflection on these stories carries the power to open up the spaces of our hearts so that we can not only welcome home the Word, but also welcome home each child. This "welcoming home" is the freedom to be inclusive in spite of differences. "Welcoming home" is a way to create a community that can be enriched by each student's personal past as well as their corporate, ethnic, and cultural experiences.

The purpose of the introductory comments and reflection questions is to assist the catechist, teacher, homilist, and liturgist to DO this "welcoming home." To reflect on the original Gospel text is to open those wide spaces within the heart and make it our own.

The procedure for using the stories can vary according to circumstances. The introduction of novelty is the true element of surprise, which makes a familiar story ever new. It is important to "fill in the blanks" with the students' help so that they are involved in the re-creation of the story. The story can be simply read to the students or used as a script for a directed pantomime, or for a dramatization. Simple signs can be used in place of scenery. After the story is acted out, it is important to do the follow-up questions and activities. Particularly important is relating the contemporary version to the original Gospel story. Helping the students discover the richness of contrasts between the stories deepens and intensifies the power of the Gospel message. The feelings of the students about the modern-day version are conformed to the past story of Gospel in a particularly relevant way. These new feelings provide a source for relating their everyday experiences to the Gospel.

CHAPTER I

The Invitation

(Luke 19:1-10)

This story comes from the fourth section of the Lucan Gospel. It is based on a thematic journeying structure. Jesus is traveling through Perea to Jerusalem for the last time. The evangelist is reflecting on what it takes to walk with Jesus on his journey. It is important to note that the sayings and parables in this portion of Luke are not found in the other three Gospel accounts and are taken from independent sources available to Luke.

There are two contrasting emotions, indignation and delight, that make the story thought-provoking. The indignation comes from the self-righteous moralism of the onlookers who have all ready judged Zaccheus and ruled out the possibility of a conversion or change of heart. Secondly, the delight with which Jesus welcomes Zaccheus into his presence is a totally unconditional initiative. Jesus engages Zaccheus and the onlookers and introduces novelty into their ordered existence. This surprise throws the believing community and Zaccheus off balance and challenges both to

change. The challenge is an invitation to re-construct a
new worldview which incorporates the creative dimension of surprise into the everyday life of both the
community and the individual.

Jesus personifies the inclusivity of the welcoming
community by sharing bread with the estranged. This
is eucharistic community at its very best.

The main issue here is how we make space for the
"wrongdoer." The Zaccheus in our life could be anyone
that we don't understand or who doesn't agree with our
way as The Way. It could be the unruly student in our
class, the new family in the neighborhood, the "con-
servative" parishioner, the undocumented worker, the
AIDS patient. This is a poignant story that commands
us to reflect critically about the opportunities each of
us has for welcoming home those who are alienated
from us.

As messengers of "welcoming home," we need to
"surprise" students with different ways of feeling, seeing, and thinking about the everyday realities that
texture their lives. We need to help them trust their own
experiences of being welcomed so that they can move
out toward others who are different. How do we do this?
By "surprising" others with our own welcoming spirit,
we actively engage our students in the process of becoming more inclusive. Surprise is the heart of the
creative advance moving in ever-widening circles. This
"surprise" is personified in Jesus' invitation to Zaccheus.

Reflection Questions
1. Who is the one student (person) in my class (life) from
   whom I feel most alienated? Why?
2. What is one good quality in that person?
3. What can I do to make a space in my heart for
   welcoming home that person?

4. How can I use my experience of this "welcoming home" to surprise others in my life?

THE INVITATION

Once upon a time there was a bill collector named _____ (name of student). The bill collector went to three families. At the first family, the bill collector said: "If you pay me $10, I will tell the _____ (bank, car company, water co.) that I didn't see you today. Then you can have more time to get your payment together."

The first family was so worried that they agreed to the bill collector's plan.

The bill collector then went to the second family and said: "If you pay me $10, I will tell the _____ (electric co., gas co., department store) that I didn't see you today. Then you can have more time to get your payment together."

The second family was so worried that they agreed to the bill collector's plan.

The bill collector then went to the third family and said: "If you pay me $10, I will tell the _____ (repossessor, rental co., refrigerator co.) that I didn't see you today. Then you can have more time to get your payment together."

The third family was so worried that they agreed to the bill collector's plan.

That day Jesus came into town. As he walked by the crowds on _____ (local street name), three groups of people shouted to him.

The first group were people who went to church every Sunday and sometimes during the week. These people helped the poor, and were good workers in the parish of _____ (name local parish). As Jesus passed they all shouted: "Have dinner at our house Jesus."

The second group were curious people standing on the corner by _____ (name of school). They were yelling at the top of their voices: "Teach us Jesus, teach us."

The third group were the families who had been cheated by the bill collector and they yelled out: "Hurray, Jesus will give us all we need."

The bill collector, hearing all the excitement, hung his head out of the second story window. He had been counting all the money he had made that week from cheating others.

As Jesus passed by, he looked up and seeing the bill collector said: "Hurry down here _____ (name of student). Tonight I'm going to have dinner at your house."

All the people who had been calling out to Jesus now became very angry and shouted: "That's not fair."

The bill collector was so surprised at the invitation from Jesus that he said: "I will not only give back the money I took, but I will give back 4 times as much from my own money."

Jesus said to the bill collector: "Today, happiness has come to your house, for I have come to find and save what was lost."

PRIMARY LEVEL

1. What is a bill collector? (someone who collects money on bills)
2. What did the bill collector do to each family? (he/she got them to pay $10 more so they could have extra time to pay)
3. When Jesus came to the twon, what did the people think he would do? (they thought he would get their money back)
4. What did the curious people want from Jesus? (they wanted Jesus to teach them)
5. What did the church people want? (they wanted Jesus to have dinner at their house)

6. Why did the people think Jesus was unfair? (he ate with the bill collector who had cheated them)
7. Why did Jesus eat at the bill collector's house? (he wanted to show him/her forgiveness)
8. How did the bill collector change? (he/she gave back the money he/she took and 4 times as much from his/her own pocket)
9. When we do wrong things how can we change? (accept any reasonable answer)

Activities
1. Draw a candle and decorate it. Give the candle to someone with whom you want to make peace.
2. In pairs act out in pantomime a time when someone forgave you.
3. Find a storytelling partner and each tell the other about a time when someone invited you to their house.

INTERMEDIATE LEVEL
1. What did the bill collector do to the families? Why? (he/she took extra money so they could have more time)
2. Who were the three groups of people in the crowds? (the curious people, the church people, those who had been cheated)
3. What did each group want? (to be taught, to have Jesus eat at their houses, to get their money back)
4. Why was Jesus' invitation to the bill collector surprising? (the bill collector had been cheating others)
5. How did the bill collector answer Jesus' invitation? Why? (he/she gave the money back and added 4 times as much from his/her own money, he/she was shocked that Jesus wanted to be his/her friend)
6. What does the story tell us about Jesus? (he loved everyone, he gave wrongdoers chances to change)

7. How can we be more like Jesus in our families, at school, and in our neighborhood? (accept any reasonable answer)
8. What is the most important lesson in the story? (to give everyone another chance)

Activities
1. Like the crowd we often dislike others. List 5 possible reasons and describe how we can change those reasons of dislike into ways of friendship.
2. Using your imagination, create a story about forgiveness that could take place in the year 2285 on the planet Mars.
3. Teaming up with a drama partner, pantomime a skit that shows someone wanting to change for the better.

JUNIOR HIGH LEVEL
1. What was the bill collector doing wrong? (he/she was taking extra money from the people)
2. What were the three groups of people and what did each want? (curious wanted to be taught, church people wanted Jesus to have dinner with them, the people who were cheated wanted justice)
3. Why is the end of the story unexpected? (the bill collector was the person who was doing wrong so you don't expect Jesus to eat with him/her)
4. Why did the crowd become angry at Jesus when he invited himself to the bill collector's for dinner? (they expected Jesus to spend time with them and not with wrongdoers)
5. In what ways do we judge what others are like? (accept any reasonable answer)
6. Why was Jesus' invitation unconditional? (he wanted to show the bill collector that he loved him/her no matter what he/she had done)

7. In our own lives how can we follow Jesus' example?
   (accept any reasonable answer)

Activities
1. Read Luke 19:1-10 and list the similarities and differences between the two stories.
2. Divide the class and debate this question: America is based on the free enterprise system. If the bill collector was clever enough to make a few extra dollars then he/she should feel that he/she did nothing wrong.
3. Research the established code of ethics involved in the following professions: medicine, law, public accounting, journalism, priesthood. Then, using your own ideas, construct your own code of ethics for a Junior High student.
4. Imagine being on a colonizing mission to a new planet. With a think-partner or on your own, describe what your idea of a successful colony would be. Then construct a set of five guidelines to help your colony be a happy environment.
5. Draw a group rainbow, each person using a different color or design for his/her band. Discuss how the contrast enriches the overall design. How is this art related to the story?

CHAPTER II

The Forgiving Parents

(Luke 15:11-32)

The "Prodigal Son" story is the welcome home
story par excellence. It is important to begin reading
this parable in the context of the entire chapter. Ap-
propriately, Luke 15 begins with two epigrammatical
metaphors for Divine Mercy. This parable has a two-
pronged focus. The theme that first catches our attention is the absolute unconditional, ever-faithful love of
the father for his son, (mother for her daughter, parents
for their children.) Secondly, the Gospel writer emphasizes the shared jubilation of homecoming. When
people make up or are reconciled, Jesus tells us what
young people know by instinct: "Let's have a party to
celebrate."

Again Jesus is involved in sharing a meal with
sinners. The scribes and pharisees, the professional
religious of his time, question Jesus. Characteristically,
he answers with a question, a question that throws the
moral dilemma back on their shoulders in a simple
experiential way. He asks them: If you had a hundred
sheep and lost one, who among you would search out

the lost one? What a wonderful question! It's the kind of question that has a hook on it. We all answer Jesus' question with a resounding "Yes," we would do the same. What then is the consequence of finding the lost sheep? Friends and neighbors are invited over to celebrate the finding of that which was lost.

This is an important issue in the role of salvation, health and wholeness, in our own lives. Other peoples' good fortune, material or spiritual, should be a source of joy to us. The brother who stayed at home and "never disobeyed" and "slaved" for his father was self-righteously indignant. He had indulged himself in the role of martyr, self-sacrificial care-taker. He had always tried to do what his parents wanted. All he felt was anger at being taken for granted. His life-long role as "victim" made him cling to what he thought should be his. He resented his father's generous forgiving spirit because he wanted what his brother was receiving. He would not make space in his heart for the joy of his brother's homecoming and the welcoming spirit of his father's generosity. The result was that he was not joyful; he made his own suffering. He was not welcoming; he made his own loneliness. His world had become his prison while he himself had the key. The key is the element of "surprise" that Jesus introduces into the story: the parent was unconditionally loving to both the prodigal and the self-righteous alike.

Reflection Questions
1. How do I share in the joy of others? Do I share my own joy with others, especially with my students and within my own family?
2. As a teacher of the Good News, do I give those whom I teach an opportunity to reflect on their family experiences? Do I provide opportunities for them to share their cultural and ethnic wealth?

3. What can I do to create a sense of belonging and family-feeling within my specific ministry?
4. Do I allow myself to feel victimized by others through the role of self-sacrificing care-taker? Do I use this as a way to control others?

THE FORGIVING PARENTS

Once upon a time a father and mother, _____ and _____ (names of students), had two children, _____ and _____ (names of students). They had a small family business _____ (Burger King, laundry etc.), and both parents worked in it. They saved their money for their children's education. One day the son said to his parents: "Please give me my share of the savings. I want to _____ (have some fun, do my own thing, live free)."

With his money the son rented a private jet from _____ (name of airlines) and left for _____ (local gambling area: Vegas, Atlantic City etc.). When he arrived he rented a _____ (expensive car name) from _____ (rental company) so he could drive around in style. He even hired a chauffeur named _____ (name of student).

When he reached _____ (hotel name), he rented the entire top floor and invited everyone he met in the streets to a party. He ordered the most expensive food _____ (name of food) and _____ (drink). For entertainment, he hired _____ (famous star) to make his new found friends happy.

He and his friends gambled and partied all night long until all his money was gone. When everyone discovered that his pockets were empty, they left him. The hotel manager threw him out, and the _____ (rental car co.) took his car away.

After two days of wandering the streets in hunger, he was hired by a _____ (pig farmer, cactus grower, chemical plant etc). After a week of loneliness and poor pay, he said to himself, "My father pays his help better than this. He decided to hitch a ride back home to his family. At least he wouldn't be so lonely and he could get a good meal. On the road he was picked up by a truck carrying _____ (manure, livestock, toxic waste) and was dropped off two blocks from his home on _____ (street name). A neighbor _____ (name of student) ran ahead to tell the son's parents that he was coming home. His parents were so excited that they ran down to the corner of _____ (name of street) by the _____ (landmark).

They said: "We're so glad to see you. Hurry home and invite your friends over so we can have a _____ (pizza, ice cream, dance) party for you."

Now the neighbor, also ran over to the family business where the son's sister was working and said: "Your brother has come home and your parents are giving a party for him and his friends."

The sister went home and heard _____ (popular song, group, or music) coming from the house. She saw her brother's friends dancing _____ (name of dance), but did not go in. Her parents came out and asked: "What's wrong? Your brother has come home and we are having a party to celebrate."

The daughter said: "I never left you, or spent my money foolishly, and have always worked in our family business. And you never gave a party for me and my friends."

"Don't you know that whatever we have is yours. Your brother was lost and gone away. Now he is found and has come home. Be happy with us."

The homecoming party was a big success. Everyone _____ (danced, played games) and ate _____ (pizza or other ethnic food, ice cream, cake).

PRIMARY LEVEL

1. Why did the parents save their money? (for their children's education)
2. Why did the son want to have his share of the money? (so he could have fun)
3. What were some of the things the son did in the gambling town? (rented a car, rented hotel floor, gave a party, had expensive food, hired entertainment)
4. Why did the son go home? (he was lonely)
5. Why was the sister not happy when her brother came home? (the son had done wrong and was given a party)
6. How did the parents welcome the son home? (they ran out to hug him and gave him a party for his friends)
7. How can we show our parents that we are sorry for doing wrong? (accept any reasonable answer)
8. Who, like our parents, always forgives us? (Jesus, God)

Activities

1. Draw a picture of your parents forgiving you and welcoming you home.
2. Draw your house and dinner table with special welcome home food on it.
3. Choose a storytelling partner and tell about a time when someone made you feel happy and at home.
4. Show the video Pinnochio after using this parable and compare the stories. Then have the students choose their own groups of three or four so they can act out a part of the Pinocchio story that is like or unlike the parable.

INTERMEDIATE LEVEL

1. Why did the son leave home? (to have fun)

2. What did he do when he was gone? (rented an expensive car, hotel room, gambled, hired famous stars)
3. Why did he go home? (he was lonely)
4. How was he greeted? (his parents ran out to meet him and gave him a party)
5. How did his sister act when he came home? (she did not welcome him because he had done wrong and had been given a party)
6. Have you ever wanted to leave home? Why? (various responses)
7. What made the son unhappy when he was away from home? (he was lonely and had no one to care for him)
8. Why did his parents give him a party? (they wanted to show their forgiveness and love)
9. Do you think his sister really loved her brother? Why or why not? (accept any reasonable answer, emphasize that she was angry because she didn't think her parents appreciated that she was doing good. This is an opportunity to help students name anger, claim it, and move through it).

Activities
1. Break into groups of four and read Luke 14:11-32. List each character and write one sentence about each person.
2. Draw a maze for the Prodigal Son to find his way home. Use the events in the story as dead ends (rented jet, gambling town, job in the city, loneliness, hunger).
3. Make a yarn outline of a treasure chest labeled HOME on the bulletin board. Then have each student draw a gift and write on the backside what home means to them.

JUNIOR HIGH LEVEL

1. Retell the story's three main points on paper either by drawing or writing. (son took the money his parents had saved and left home, he spent it all and was lonely, he returned and was welcomed with a party)
2. Why did the son leave home? (he wanted to have fun, to be independent)
3. Why didn't his sister go into the house until her parents came out? (she was angry and hurt because she had been loyal to her parents and they had never given her a party)
4. Were the people that the son met really his friends? Why or why not? (when his money ran out they left him)
5. What was the sister's relationship with her brother? (accept any reasonable answer)
6. Were the parents fair in giving the party for someone who had done wrong and spent all their hardearned money? (opinion answer)
7. How do you know who your real friends are? (accept any reasonable answer, emphasize loyalty even when things are hard)
8. What is forgiveness according to the story? Do you agree? (unconditional acceptance with no questions asked)

Activities
1. Read Luke 15:11-32 and list the similarities and differences between the two stories.
2. Write and then act out an interview, as a TV talk show host, with any one of the characters in the story.
3. Write an argumentative essay (pro or con) on the topic: "Material Wealth Brings Happiness."
4. List two real friends and tell why each is your friend and then write thank you notes to them.

5. Working in a collaborative team, role play a family situation in which forgiving and understanding are the themes.
6. Choose a think-partner. Discuss whether money is necessary or not and try to construct alternative ways for creating a society without money.
7. Plan a forgiveness prayer celebration followed by a party that includes sharing food, music, and dancing.

CHAPTER III

The Gift

(Luke 21:1-4)

This Gospel story should be read in the context of Chapters 20 and 21. Within this framework Luke describes the continuing concern of the professional religious about Jesus' authority. Dissent from traditional, official teaching was viewed by some as a threat. Luke shows this threat to be a question of Jesus' growing influence and power. The people came to hear him speak in the temple (Lk 21:38).

Jesus also made it clear, in his daily teaching, that the scribes were living well at the expense of the poor. He was questioning both the community's acceptance of injustice and the individual hypocrisy of the religious leaders. His prophetic warning, addressed to his disciples within the hearing of the people, is also a challenge to his followers for continual conversion and sincerity of heart (Lk 20:46-47). Jesus points out that many of the professional religious were growing wealthy through the savings of widows. They took the front seats in the synagogues and banquets and made a show of their prayer life.

Jesus endangers the self-interest of the religious power structure and creates a vision of justice which embodies compassion. Luke places the story of the Widow's Mite in this setting and it is powerful.

The institutional religious are looking for ways to entrap Jesus. They want to discredit the prophetic dimension in his teaching by questioning his authority. Jesus does not claim this authority for himself. Rather, it is how he lives and the justice of what he says that moves the people to belief. He just doesn't talk about how others should live, but his actions are his word. For Jesus, this coming to oneness or personal integrity is his very relationship with God as parent.

Luke portrays Jesus as a storyteller who sees through the pretense of the rich (Luke 21:1). Here, giving is shown in its truest sense. It is not a matter of quantity, but intention. Those who are concerned about the external appearances of their giving are motivated by self-interest. They hope to be recognized as generous. This kind of giving is not giving at all and has no effect on the "giver." On the other hand, Jesus sees the gift of the widow who gives what she cannot afford as the true measure of generosity. Her gift affects her profoundly because she has chosen to trust that her needs will be met.

Often because of "burn-out," we feel that we are giving more than what we have. We identify ourselves with the widow because it is not out of our extra that we are giving. Yet, to be "burned out" is to set ourselves over against ourselves. We are not at one with ourselves, and, consequently, cannot be in harmony with others. We cannot relax enough to trust more than just ourselves. We do not want to need others. Yet, the essential nature of community is both interdependence and personal integrity.

As teachers of the Gospel, we are not just a group of rugged individualists "graced" with indomitable personal charisma and unflagging commitment. Grace is a gift of strength in weakness, not strength without weakness. Our gifts are not just for ourselves. They are for the growth of the community, growth in two ways: First as a growing inward and outward; second, as a growing toward creative unity. This Gospel-centered unity is different from sameness. Jesus clearly points this out in his attack on the self-righteous certainty of his critics. This Gospel-centered unity opens up space for the creative gifts of all. As teachers, with both our individual gifts and personal commitment, we can create an environment that encourages the inclusion of cultural and ethnic diversity as sources of wealth not weakness. This inclusive community, characterized by Luke through Jesus' concern for the widow, is the challenge of "welcoming home" the weak and powerless so they can claim their own power.

Reflection Questions
1. When do I feel most tired and discouraged? Why?
2. How can I show others that I both need them and respect their personal integrity?
3. How can I help others in ministry transform their feelings of "burn-out" into feelings of trust?
4. How can I be more compassionate to the lives of others and accept the weaknesses in myself? How can I use this compassion to believe in others and in myself?

THE GIFT

Once upon a time there were three children who lived in ____ (name of city) on ____ (local street name) just around the corner from ____ (school name). ____

(name of student) was 5 years old, _____ (name of student) was 12 years old, and _____ (name of student) was 16 years old. Their father said: "This Christmas (birthday, holiday or other special occasion) we are all going to surprise your mother with _____ (children select a present). So let's all try to save our money and then put it all together."

All three children were excited. _____, the 16 year old, worked part-time after school at _____ (Burger King, car wash etc.) and saved $20 from his extra money.

_____, the 12 year old, took an extra _____ (babysitting, lawn mowing, etc.) job and saved $10.

_____, the 5 year old tried to save part of his lunch money every day, but on the way home he lost what he had saved.

Their father said: "Let's put our money together and see how much we have."

_____ (16 year old) came up and said: "I saved $20 from working at _____ (local place)."

_____ (12 year old) came up and said: "I saved $10 from my extra _____ job."

_____ (5 year old) came up and said: "I tried to save some lunch money, but I lost it on the way home and all I have left is a penny."

The other children laughed. But their father said to the youngest:

"Your brother and sister gave out of the extra money they had, but you gave everything, even to the last penny."

PRIMARY LEVEL
1. How many children were there and how old were they? (three children—5 years, 12 years, 16 years)
2. What did the father want them to do? (save their money for a present for their mother)

3. How did each one save their money? (oldest worked part-time, 12 year old worked an extra job, youngest saved part of his lunch money)
4. How much did each save? (oldest $20, middle $10, youngest lost all but a penny)
5. Why did the older children laugh at the youngest? (he only had a penny)
6. Was the father happy with what the youngest gave? Why?(he gave all he had)
7. What does selfish mean? (accept any reasonable answer)

Activities
1. Read Luke 21:1-4, the Widow's Mite, and ask the children who is like the widow in the story "The Gift."
2. Make "I Love You" cards for your parents showing that a gift can be simple and cost nothing.
3. Each child make a Care Flower and give it to someone in another class, saying to them: "This is a gift."

INTERMEDIATE LEVEL
1. What did the father suggest that the children do? (save money for a present for their mother)
2. How did each save some money? (oldest took a part-time job, middle took an extra job, youngest saved lunch money)
3. Why did the older children laugh? (the youngest had lost everything but a penny)
4. What did the father say? (the other two had given their extra money, but the youngest gave all he had left)
5. What is a gift? (accept any reasonable answer, but emphasize that a gift is given without expecting anything in return)

6. Why did the father praise the youngest? (he gave all he had. The other two gave more because they could earn more)
7. What other kinds of gifts are there? (love, being cared for, friendship, understanding)
8. What are some of the ways in which we can give gifts in our family, school, and neighborhood? (doing good, accept any reasonable answer)
9. Why is the reason for giving a gift important? (because you could want something in return, emphasize the motive)

Activities
1. Cut out a heart and print one gift you have been given. On the back write a Thank You prayer. Use them on a THANKFULNESS bulletin board with the hearts as a bouquet of flowers on a holiday (Thanksgiving) table.
2. Go to a younger grade and retell the story.
3. Read Luke 21:1-4 and list all the similarities and differences in the two stories.
4. Choose a storytelling partner and share a time in your life when you were surprised with a gift. Describe how you felt, who the gift giver was, and how you showed that the gift made you happy.

JUNIOR HIGH LEVEL
1. How did each child save money? (part-time work, an extra job, lunch money)
2. Why did the older children laugh? (accept any reasonable answer)
3. Do you think the father appreciated the older children's contribution? Can you tell from the story? (accept any reasonable answer)
4. Read the Widow's Mite (Luke 21:1-4). How are the widow and the youngest alike? (they both gave more than just what was extra and not needed)

5. Why didn't the father in "The Gift" or Jesus in "The Widow's Mite" thank the people who gave more? (the point of the story emphasizes giving more than just what is extra)
6. Isn't the contributions of thousands of dollars to the poor more important than a few dollars? (emphasize the motive and circumstances of the giving)
7. What is a gift? (something given with no strings attached out of love)

Activities
1. Write a short skit about gift giving and act it out for the class.
2. After reading Psalms 147:7-9, Psalms 138:1-6 write your own psalm of Thanksgiving.
3. Read O'Henry's *Gift of the Magi* and compare what gift giving means in this story to the "Widow's Mite" and "The Gift."
4. Using the name of a friend, write an acrostic describing the talents and gifts of the person. Then, if you want, give it to that person.
5. Imagine a gift for the world and draw a symbol for it. Write how this gift would change your personal life.
6. Think of gifts in creation and how they affect your life. Imagine each gift as a shape and color. Share your image- ings with another person.

CHAPTER IV

The Guests

(Luke 10:38-41)

The story of Martha and Mary follows the Good Samaritan parable. Martha is busy with the details involved with the customary duties of hospitality. She asks Jesus why he is not concerned about Mary letting her do all the work. It seems that Martha wants Jesus to rebuke Mary publicly. She wants to be in control of the situation by being the self-sacrificing care-taker.

Jesus' response is direct. He reproaches Martha by calling into question her motivation. The duties of hospitality have made her upset and anxious. She can't relax because the harsh expectations she has placed on herself overflow and destroy the relaxation of everyone else. To Martha appearances seem to be more important than welcoming. A kind of obsessive perfectionism hinders Martha's ability to let others be who they are. Jesus says simply that only one thing is required. He doesn't say specifically what that is, but he does say that Mary has chosen rightly.

Mary, on the other hand, sits at Jesus' feet and listens. She is in the company of the apostles as one who comes to learn from Jesus; and, in learning from him, she serves him just as surely as does Martha. This kind of attentiveness breaks with the traditional role of women and their social function as manager of ritualistic details. Mary, unconcerned about appearances and traditional roles, chooses the better part. What is this better part? Jesus never says directly. Yet, his actions question the traditional ways of doing things. He "lures" his listeners to feel and think about social, cultural, and religious customs in new ways. It is this liberation from appearances, stereotypes, and roles which Jesus offers as a universal appeal for understanding others on a deeper level. Martha's anxiety about how things should be have only created division, tension, and disharmony.

As teachers involved in various programs and ministries, it is often easy to judge success by appearances: the number of students in our classes or people at our worship services, how well they respond, how we are accepted or appreciated. These externals too often become the support system on which we depend. In this Lucan story Jesus is questioning our priorities. What actually does get our attention? Is it the details of our ministry or is it the individual person to whom we minister? How do we judge success? Is it by the number of people we affect or is it by the quality of time that we share with others?

Reflection Questions
1. Do I judge my students (others) by their achievements and their willingness to work hard? How do I feel toward those who seem to put little effort into their work?
2. What kind of activities do I provide so that each student can experience some feeling of success?

3. With whom have I spent quality time in the last week? Or have my personal contacts been primarily superficial?

THE GUESTS

Every Sunday at 2:00 Grandma _____ (name of student) and Grandpa _____ (name of student) came to visit their grandchildren, _____ and _____ (names of students). As their _____ (kind of car) came down _____ (street name), the children's dog, _____ (dog's name) recognized the sound of their car and barked. The children ran to the door with open arms. Grandpa would ask _____ (name of child): "Have you been a good boy this week?" He always answered, "Yes, Grandpa." His grandfather would give him _____ (amount of money) for his weekly allowance, which he would save carefully.

"Have you worked hard this week," he would ask _____ (name of other child).

"Yes, Grandpa," she would answer. Grandfather would give her _____ (amount of money) for her weekly allowance, which she spent on candy and ice cream.

_____ (name of saver) always helped the mother in the kitchen with dinner. _____ (name of spender) always sat and listened to Grandpa's stories about _____ (experiences suited to geographic area).

Suddenly, one Sunday _____ (saver) became angry and said: "_____ (spender), can't you ever help in the kitchen? I always help mother with the work. Grandpa won't you tell her to help me?"

But the grandfather said: "Why are you so upset and angry? If _____ (spender) wants to listen to the stories, that's OK too."

PRIMARY LEVEL

1. Who came to dinner every Sunday? (the grand-parents)
2. What did the grandfather ask every week? (if they had been good)
3. What did he give them? (a weekly allowance)
4. What did the two children do with it? (one saved it and the other spent it on candy and ice cream)
5. When the grandparents visited what did the two children do? (one helped in the kitchen and the other listened to the grandfather's stories)
6. Why did the helper get angry? (his sister wasn't helping in the kitchen)
7. How did the children show their love for their grand-parents? (one helped, one listened)
8. What are some of the ways you can help your mother at home when visitors come? (emphasize that there are a variety of ways to help, being a good listener is one way also)

Activities
1. Choose a storytelling partner and share a time when you were a good helper when you had guests.
2. Draw a picture of a family party and share with the class how each person helps make your family a happy family.
3. Using tempera, paint one foot and make a footprint on a roll of paper. Use it as a welcome banner saying: "Step Right In! Welcome To Our Class." Label each footprint with the child's name.

INTERMEDIATE LEVEL

1. Who came to visit every Sunday? (the grandparents)
2. What did the children do to make that day special for their grandparents? (one helped in the kitchen, one listened to the grandfather's stories)

3. Why was the helper angry? (he felt that listening was not helping)
4. When can listening be helping at home and at school? (when others need help, directions being given, friendship)
5. Read LK 10:38-41. How are the two stories alike?
6. How can we make guests feel welcome at home and school? (accept any reasonable answer)

Activities
1. Make a guest book for your classroom by pasting a picture of each student on construction paper with a welcome note from each student.
2. Choose a storytelling partner in a primary grade and retell the story of "The Guest."
3. Welcome another class, principal, or teacher into your room. Then pantomime the story as it is being read. Have a celebration of hospitality with a welcome blessing for your guests written by your class.

JUNIOR HIGH LEVEL
1. Read LK 10:38-41 and discuss how the two stories are alike and different.
2. Why did the helper become angry? (the other child was not helping)
3. Did the one helping in the kitchen have a good reason to be upset? (Bring out the fact that the child was judging the other. Each child was helping in their own way.)
4. Discuss the proverb in Proverbs 21:2 and its relationship to the parable (either the modern one or the Gospel story).

Activities
1. Using the proverb in Proverbs 20:3 discusss how it relates to the parable. Then in groups of 2 or 3 act out a skit that illustrates the proverb's message.

2. Using the Book of Proverbs, find a proverb, write a paragraph about its meaning, and illustrate it on construction paper.
3. With a think-partner discuss ways in which people are welcomed or not welcomed. Write a skit to act out both situations. Invite others to join in presenting the play.
4. Plan an imaginary dinner party and invite any ten great people, living or dead, past or present. Tell why you invited these particuar people. Then join with another person, choose one dinner guest from each list and write an imaginary conversation between them. Using a tape recorder, read your dialogue with expression and play it for the class.

CHAPTER V

The Lost Kitten

(Luke 15:1-10)

Jesus is questioned about sharing a meal with sinners and tax collectors. He confronts the exclusivity of his critics with two images, the lost coin and the lost sheep from Ezekiel 34:11-16. Jesus, in this parable, strongly states that his mission is to save, to bring to health and wholeness, those who are excluded from the believing community. Jesus describes for us the energy of a perservering goodness which remains always unconditioned, never excluding but always including. This uniting energy of salvation does two things. First, it reconciles what is separated from the community. This active forgiveness initiates and completes the ongoing moment-by-moment process of bringing the alienated into the ever-widening circle of God's life-giving love. Secondly, it liberates both the alienated and the community for rejoicing. Both have been saved from "lostness" and healed for a wider uniting, a deeper rejoicing. In Ezekiel, the intensity of this joy has its source in God. God rescues the sheep from ruthless, self-satisfied shepherds who were appointed to tend them (34:10). The

prophet articulates God's complaints them with sharp-
ness and poignance (Ez 34:3-5). He accuses them of
being brutal and harsh with the sheep. They wore their
wool, drank their milk, and slaughtered the fatlings.
They did not care for the sick and weak of the flock;
and when the strays wandered off, the shepherds aban-
doned them. Since the shepherds who were appointed
used the sheep for their own comfort, instead of caring
for them, God appoints one shepherd (34:23). This
shepherd is chosen not as someone to "be in charge,"
but to continue God's "welcoming home." This is the
re-creative activity of a God who in every moment
welcomes home God's own people. It is a powerful
reconciliation for both the "lost" and the community.
The individual cannot be separated from the community nor the community from the individual. They
are interdependent and effect the character of the
whole. The many who are diverse do become one; and
this one community is more than just the sum of its
members. The Lucan account echoes Ezekiel who describes this unifying possibility in our own lives as
coming from God's own reconciling activity (34:13-16).
It is God's activity in our everyday world that creates
a surprising newness in the midst of a community who
open their hearts to welcome the different, the marginalized. This unity of spirit within the witnessing
community is always being increased by One. This
"added" One is God's healing activity and saving presence in the life of the faithful community.

As teachers who feel called, Ezekiel's indictment
of the shepherds' breech of trust and Luke's challenge
to the true nature of community poses a felt tension in
our ministry. Yet, we must always realize that we are
not doing it alone. It does not all depend on us. It is
always the "added" One who teaches us how to be
faithful to the message of "welcoming home." This is

the source of our hope and encourages us to develop a sense of humor. If mistakes disrupt us so that we brood about them instead of learn from them, then we are forgetting who really is in charge.

If we become preoccupied about how a program works instead of how the people are being engaged and empowered, then we are in danger of taking ourselves too seriously.

Reflection Questions
1. How do I feel about my prayer life? What is my prayer life like?
2. How do I feel God active in my life?
3. How do I show others that God's reconciliating power makes a difference in how I live my life?
4. What are the things in my ministry that I take too seriously? How can I change this? How often do I laugh, socialize, or play with others?

THE LOST KITTEN

Once upon a time there was a mother cat named _____ (students name it) and her five kittens. They lived in a patio at the _____ (family name) house on _____ (name of street).

Every day for six weeks _____ and _____ (names of students) watched the mother cat feed her kittens. Then one morning, before the children went to _____ school (name of school), a large _____ (breed of dog) jumped over the fence and scared the cat family in all directions.

The next day was Saturday. The children loved Saturday because they watched their favorite TV shows in the morning and played all afternoon and had _____ (favorite food) for dinner. They watched _____ and _____ (TV shows). This Saturday, however, was different. They didn't want to watch TV. Instead they went out looking for the kittens. They found all but one of the kittens. Walking down _____ (street name) they searched high and low. They looked in all the _____ (kind of tree) and under all the cars: _____ and _____ (types of cars), but they still could not find the lost kitten. They spent their whole Saturday looking. When it began to get dark, _____ said to _____ (names of students): "It's getting dark. We should be getting home before mom and dad begin to worry."

So the children sadly walked down _____ (street) to their house. When their parents saw how sad they were they said: "Now it's our turn to go out and look for the lost kitten."

The parents looked up and down _____ (street) and even in the back alleys of _____ (local area) until they found the lost kitten.

When they brought the kitten home, the children said: "Hurray! You found the kitten. Let's have a party."

PRIMARY LEVEL
1. What scared the cat family? (a dog)
2. What did the children usually do on Saturdays? (watch TV, play, and have their favorite food)
3. How many kittens did the children find? (all but one)
4. Who finally found the lost kitten? (their parents)
5. What did they do to celebrate finding the lost kitten? (they had a party)
6. Why didn't the children watch their favorite TV programs? (they looked for the lost kitten)
7. Why did the children go home before finding the kitten? (it was getting dark and they didn't want to worry their parents)

8. Why did the parents go out to find the kitten? (they loved their children and wanted to make them happy)
9. Why do we take care of our pets? (because we care for them)
10. How do our parents take care of us? (accept any reasonable answer)

Activities
1. Tell the story of the Lost Sheep (LK 15:1-10). Explain to the children how the parents are like Jesus, the Good Shepherd (JN 10:11-18).
2. Draw a picture that shows your parents caring for you. Write a thank you note on the back and have the children take it home.
3. Draw a picture of your pets and then share a story about them with a storytelling partner.

INTERMEDIATE LEVEL
1. Read LK 15:1-10 and discuss how the two stories are alike and different.
2. Why did the children change their Saturday schedule of morning TV and afternoon play? (so they could find the kitten)
3. Why did the parents look for the kitten? (accept any reasonable answer)
4. Read JN 10:11-18. In the Lost Kitten story who is like the Good Shepherd? Why? (the parents because they searched until they found the kitten)
5. When we lose a friend how can we act more like Jesus? (we can try to make up and be friends again)
6. How can we be responsible for the pets we have? (feed them, care for them)

Activities
1. With a think-partner, make want ads for something precious that has been lost. Describe it and offer a reward (it cannot be money).
2. Write a TV news flash giving details about someone or something that is lost. Then act it out.
3. Be a talk show host interviewing any one of the characters from any or all of the three related stories: LK 15:1- 10, JN 10:11-18, or the "Lost Kitten."

JUNIOR HIGH LEVEL
1. Read LK 15:1-10 and JN 10:11-18. List the similarities with the "Lost Kitten" story. (emphasize the quality of mercy as finding that which is lost)
2. In LK 15 to whom was Jesus telling the story? Why? (the pharisees because they were criticizing him for eating with sinners)
3. From the stories what does it mean to show mercy? (emphasize that mercy is unconditional love)
4. What does "lost" mean in the story? (to be away from home or any other acceptable answer)
5. How can we show mercy in our lives? (accept any reasonable answer that emphasizes being welcoming to those who seem not to belong to a group, i.e., lost)
6. In LK 15 what lesson was Jesus teaching by using the parable of the Lost Sheep? (that mercy is finding that which is lost)
7. With whom does Mother Teresa of India work and why are they considered a lost cause? How is this like the Good Shepherd? (she works with the dying to show God's love and mercy even in the last hours of life)
8. Make a list of all those who might be considered lost or away from home. How could each be helped? What can the class as a whole or the student as an individual do to help those who are alienated?

Activities

1. In 1985 there were over 4,000 teenage runaways in Hollywood, CA, alone. In your research, find out from your city government if your city or neighborhood has a problem and what agencies provide assistance for them. Report back to the class.
2. Choose debate teams and discuss the statement: Teenage runaways are delinquents.
3. Divide the class into groups of four and have them organize a skit about showing mercy in their lives.
4. Find out more about Mother Teresa of India, Martin Luther King, Mahatma Gandhi, Oscar Romero, and Desmond Tutu. How did they work for seeming lost causes? Present what you have found out about them by acting out an interview on a TV talk show.
5. Find a psalm in the Book of Psalms that expresses the feelings of gratitude for mercy. Then write your own psalm.

CHAPTER VI

The Loving Neighbor

(Luke 10:25-37)

The Good Samaritan parable is a response to the lawyer's question about the requirements for everlasting life. (LK 10:25). This question was of particular importance to Luke's gentile audience. How were the newly evangelized to understand salvation? Was it based on appropriation of cultural and ethnic patterns and mere repetition of Jewish tradition? Or did Jesus bring something novel to the tradition of his ancestors and his personal past? Luke's message embodies a coming-together of the gentile world, shaped by the Greek cultural past, and the Jewish tradition as interpreted by Jesus. In light of both his own Jewish tradition and his love for the essence of the law, Jesus encourages the lawyer to answer the question he asks by asking him what is written in the law. The lawyer naturally responds by quoting the heart of Jewish law (Lev 19:18, Dt 6:5): To love God with all your heart and mind and love your neighbor as yourself.

Jesus validates the lawyer's answer and encourages him to now go out and live the law he himself knows so well. However, the lawyer needs to pose another question to justify why he asked the first. He wants to know who his neighbor is. (LK 10:29) Jesus creates a classic story in which he never provides an answer for the lawyer. Answers can either be blindly accepted or easily rejected merely because of the authority of the speaker. Jesus doesn't want to let his listeners off the hook by providing easy answers to questions they already know within themselves. He uses the power of the story to effect a "truth-experience" based on the cultural context of the listener, not on his own authority as a teacher. Jesus helps the lawyer draw from his own understanding of the law and find the answer within himself.

As teachers of the Gospel, we can oftentimes succumb to the temptation of taking ourselves more seriously than the message we teach. Our answers can be given too readily. Perhaps, we feel called to proclaim a truth that we consider to be outside of our listeners, some "thing" we have to give to them, not something we are and some interior truth they know already within themselves. It is Jesus' final challenge that puts his message into perspective for us as contemporary Christians. He says to the lawyer and to every listener in all three times—past, present, and future—Go and do the same (LK 10:37).

To live the message of the compassionate Samaritan is what we need to do for salvation, health, and wholeness. This health is not just "something to have" as an individual, but it is a dynamic, ever-widening, spiralling circle of acting which includes others despite their differentness. Health is wholeness, personally and communally. The one includes the many and is enriched by the contrasts that the many provide. This dynamic interdependence creates an environment for more growth, mutual understanding, and social justice.

That Jesus uses the Samaritan as the third person in the story is a powerful "surprise," which breaks into the dominant cultural, religious, and ethnic exclusivity of his time. The priest and levite who pass the injured person represent this dominant way of thinking and acting. The shock element in the story is powerful for two reasons. First, in distinction to the professional religious who hurried passed, the Samaritan was "just" a lay person. Secondly, the Samaritan was despised because he belonged to a group who were racially mixed and religiously heretical. To be an outsider is a feeling we think we will never forget, yet it is an experience easily forgotten when we become a part of a community or in-group.

Interestingly, this particular parable is preceded by a passage that describes the inhospitality of a Samaritan town. Dominated by the cultural and religious patterns of their corporate past, the Samaritans refuse to allow Jesus and his followers to pass through their village on the journey to Jerusalem. When James and John want to call fire down to destroy the Samaritans, Jesus reprimands them (LK 9:51-55). Revenge, meanness of spirit, or smallness of heart is in no way a part of Jesus' message. It is in this light that the Lucan Gospel creates a paradigm for dealing with the difficulties and injustices in our own lives. When meanness of spirit or apparent injustice seems to be inflicted on us, we are quick to anger and revenge, sadness and self-pity. Yet, how uncharacteristic of the Galilean vision that continues to challenge us to a more radical openness, a more awakened compassion.

Reflection Questions
1. Which groups or kinds of people do I feel most different from, or antagonistic toward?

2. What positive action can I take to overcome my feelings of antagonism, mistrust, and fear?
3. When have I recently felt that others have been unjust, mean-spirited, or insensitive to me? How did I respond?
4. How do I show others that I act inclusively and not exclusively?

THE LOVING NEIGHBOR

Once upon a time _____ (name of student) from _____ (name of school) decided to catch the bus home to _____ (street name) because his/her parents were late to pick him/her up. As he/she waited at the bus stop, (gang members, muggers, etc.) attacked him/her, stole his/her bus money and books, and left him/her there.

In a few minutes, _____ (name of well-known preacher) had a meeting with _____ (name of pastor) to discuss _____ (current issue). When she passed the bus stop she said:

"O my goodness, this person is hurt, but I am late for my meeting. I don't have time to help."

In another part of the city, the new mayor _____ (name of student) called his limousine and drove down _____ (street) to _____ (local area in need of help) where the mayor was making a thank you speech to the people who just voted him into office. As his limo passed the bus stop, he said to his chauffeur _____ (name of student):

"O my goodness, this person is hurt, but I am late for my meeting. I don't have time to help."

Then a (bag lady, skid row resident etc.), while collecting aluminum cans from the streets, passed by the bus stop and said:

"O my goodness, this person is hurt. I'll see if I can help." So the (bag lady, skid row resident etc.) helped

_____ (student) to the nearest hospital _____ (name of hospital), and said to the nurse:

"I found this person on the street. Please take care of him/her. Here is all the money I have. I'll come back tomorrow to see how he/she is."

Now of the three, who do you think was the loving neighbor?

PRIMARY LEVEL
1. What did the student do after school instead of waiting for his/her parents? (decided to take the bus home)
2. Who hurt the student and why? (will vary according to the fill-in choice)
3. Why didn't the preacher of the Word of God stop to help? (she had a meeting)
4. Why didn't the mayor stop to help? (he had to give a thank you speech to those who voted for him)
5. Who did stop to help? (will vary)
6. How did the third person help the injured person? (took to the hospital, gave all the money, said he/she would be back)
7. Who, of the three, acted most like a loving neighbor? (the third because he/she helped)
8. If your parents do not come on time what should you do? (accept any reasonable answer)
9. If Jesus would have seen the hurt student, what would he have done? (he would have helped)
10. Who in the story acted most like Jesus? (the third person)
11. How can we be a loving neighbor at school or at home? (accept any reasonable answer)

Activities
1. Have each student draw a picture of themselves as they help someone at home or at school.

2. Have the students role play a time when they helped someone.
3. Make a Loving Neighbor Garden bulletin board. Every time someone acts like a loving neighbor add a flower with the child's name on it to the garden.

INTERMEDIATE LEVEL

1. What happened in the story? (a brief re-telling of the story)
2. Why didn't the first two people help the student? (accept any reasonable answer)
3. Why don't you expect the third person to be the one that helps? (the person is poor, they don't seem like they would help)
4. Tell about someone who has acted like a loving neighbor to you?
5. List the ways that you can act like a loving neighbor at home, at school, and in your neighborhood.
6. What story is this like in the Bible? (the Good Samaritan)
7. How is the story different from the Good Samaritan? (the people are modern, or any reasonable answer)
8. What are the things that make a loving neighbor? (being helpful, friendly, caring)

Activities

1. Pair up and, using any TV program, role play a brief scene that shows someone acting like a loving neighbor.
2. Trace both hands on construction paper. Decorate and write two things you can do to act like a loving neighbor. Make a Giving Tree bulletin board and, using the hands as leaves, decorate the board.
3. Have the students go into a lower grade class and re-tell the story of the Loving Neighbor.

JUNIOR HIGH LEVEL
1. From this story what do you think a parable is? (a story that exemplifies an ethical attitude or teaches a lesson. Note: This traditional literary definition is useful but a more critical theological approach is offered by John Dominic Crossan's *In Parables*, New York: Harper & Row Publishers, 1973.)
2. Why do you think Jesus used parables? (to help us learn to choose for ourselves, to interest us in his teaching, or other possible answers with an emphasis on development of conscious or inner judgment.)
3. Why does Jesus ask who the loving neighbor is instead of telling his listeners in LK 10:25-37? (so we can choose.)
4. Why is the third choice the most unlikely person? (because of the three it would seem the other two would value people more)gn
5. What do you usually assume are the values of each of the three? (minister would value justice, God's word, and Jesus' example; mayor would value justice for all citizens; third would seem too poor to care about anything.)
6. How do these expected values differ from each person's behavior? (each person that is expected to be helpful is not. The third, who would be expected to be a loner, becomes the person who helps)
7. What is a stereotype? Why are they unfair? (stereotype is a general, over-simplified mental picture about another race, religion, country, event, issue, or person. They are unfair because they are judgments made uncritically and usually based on a particular bias or prejudice without consideration being given to specific circumstances or individual differences.)

Activities

1. With a think-partner, read the original parable in Luke. Then list the ways in which the story is different and similar to the Good Samaritan.
2. In a collaborative group, list the three characters and under each name describe how your group expects each to act. Re-write the story using three different characters and a different situation.
3. In debate groups, discuss the pros and cons of these statements:

   All homeless people choose to live on the streets.

   People on welfare are lazy.

   (Point out that these statements reinforce destructive and judgmental stereotypes.)

4. Find out from local social welfare agencies or members of the city council these facts:

   a. How many homeless are in your city?

   b. Where can they find housing?

   c. What agencies provide those services that help the homeless?

   d. How can your class help?

5. In a group, brainstorm all the choices you made within the last 24 hours. Separate them into these categories: self, others, God. Draw lines from one category to another based on how your decisions influence each other.

CHAPTER VII

The Party

(Luke 18:9-14;14:7-11)

The first parable (LK 18:9-14) about the pharisee and the tax collector personifies the epigram that concludes the story (18:14). Here humility is portrayed as seeing the truth about oneself without delusion or self-justification. The tax collector acknowledges the wrongdoing that characterizes his profession. He does not make monetary reparation as required, but only asks for mercy.

On the other hand, the professional religious makes a show of his external religious observance (fasting and tithing). He feels justified in his pride as perhaps we can become justified in our own ministry within the Church. Religious externals have become ends in themselves, and are not seen as a means to God. They are not God.

In the second parable, Luke places Jesus at the house of the pharisee on the sabbath. Noticing how everyone was scrambling to get a place of honor, he tells the parable of the wedding party. In the story, the guest sits in a place of honor, only to be asked by the host to make way for another person of greater dignity. The story shows the guest's self-importance for exactly what it is.

Oftentimes in ministry this kind of self-importance is a way to help us believe that WE are the ones who are doing everything. We make ourselves indispensable. This thinking leads to an individualistic ethic, which in ministry destroys the necessity of collaborative efforts. The sense of "I must change the world" is in contradistinction to the communal nature of Jesus' message. It creates the kind of unhealthy tension in our lives that drains us of energy and joy. In other words, we take ourselves too seriously. We cannot let go of the need to change others. We do not believe that Jesus empowers others to change themselves and our job is simply to accept them the way they are, loving them unconditionally.

Occasionally, when we reflect on God's word, we think just about ourselves in a very private way. We separate our relationship with God from our relationship with others and our world. In Jesus's stories, we are called to see everything as related and interdependent while retaining personal integrity. Young people know this intuitively because they love to socialize. Life is interaction.

Through this communal dimension in the Christian experience, Jesus "surprises" his followers by serving them instead of expecting to be served (JN 13:1-17). This is the truth of humility being lived out. In serving others, Jesus shows us a kind of vulnerability that is a new vision of strength. He surprises us by turning accepted custom upside down. Jesus de-absolutizes and re-interprets the religious and social ritual of his day; and in this reinterpretation he uses his prophetic voice to challenge our own accepted ways of doing things.

To be self-important is to deny how interdependent we really are. To see ourselves in isolation as separate things or cogs in a great cosmic machine is to be blinded to the most powerful gift of the Jesus-life in us. This gift is the power to be inclusive in our love. It is the network of social interactions and human experiences in our lives that give us a sense of individual identity. We are becoming, in every moment, the person we are meant to be. It is an adventure of becoming.

Reflection Questions
1. How do I serve my students when we celebrate?
2. What opportunities do I provide for my students to serve each other?
3. What are the ways in which my students influence me?
4. How does their influence make me a more faithful follower of Jesus' word?

THE PARTY

Two students, _____ and _____, were invited to a party. One of the students was wealthy and lived in _____ (wealthy part of town). The other student was poor and lived near _____ (poorer section).

_____, the wealthy child, stood next to his/her friend _____ and said:

"My father brought me here in his new _____ (expensive kind of car). Look at that boy/girl over there. He/she came in a _____ (year and less expensive model car.)" _____, the poor student, stood off in the corner and thought:

"Everyone is dressed so nicely. I only have these _____ (kind of clothes or shoes)." _____ (wealthy student) said to his/her friend in a loud voice:

"My mother bought me this new ____ (kind of clothes) for the party. I'm glad I'm not like most of these kids and especially that boy/girl over there."

When the ____ (kind of food) was being served, ____ (wealthy student) hurried over to sit near the guest of honor. But ____ (guest of honor) saw ____ (poor student) standing off in the corner and said to him/her:

"Come over here and sit next to me, so you can enjoy the party too."

PRIMARY LEVEL

1. Who was invited to the party? (a wealthy student and a poor student)
2. What did the wealthy student say to his/her friend? (his/her father brought him/her in a new car)
3. Why did the wealthy student say he/she wasn't like the rest of the students at the party? (he/she had nicer clothes)
4. How did the poor student feel? Why? (sad because he/she didn't have nice clothes)
5. What does "guest of honor" mean? (the person who is having the party)
6. Why did the wealthy student hurry to sit by the guest of honor? (he/she wanted to be first, or he/she thought he/she was special)
7. Who did the guest of honor ask to sit next to him/her? Why? (the poor student, he/she wanted him/her to enjoy him/herself)
8. Who made the poor student feel welcome at the party? How? (the guest of honor because he/she invited him/her to sit next to him/her)
9. Who in the story acted most like Jesus? Why? (the guest of honor because he/she wanted everyone to have fun and he/she noticed the poor student)
10. How can we make others feel welcome at our school? (by sharing with them, playing with them)

11. How do your parents show you that you are special to them? (loving, caring, protecting,, feeding, clothing)

Activities
1. Choose an acting partner and pretend you are welcoming each other to a party.
2. Make a Thank-You Flower for your parents. On each petal write something you are thankful for and then color it. Give it to your parents tonight at dinner.
3. Make a Welcome-Picture of something at your school that makes it a family. Then put them into a guest book for visitors.

PRIMARY LEVEL
1. How were the wealthy student and the poor student different? (they came in different cars, had different clothes, behaved differently)
2. Why did the wealthy student hurry to the guest of honor? (he/she wanted to sit next to him/her)
3. Why did the wealthy student speak loudly? (various answers, he/she wanted others to know what he/she had)
4. Why did the poor student stand in the corner? (he/she was embarrassed about his/her clothes)
5. Was the end of the story a surprise? Why?
6. Who in the story acted like Jesus would act? Why? (the guest of honor because he/she wanted everyone to have fun)
7. Read LK 18:9-14. How are the two stories similar? How are they different?
8. What was the prayer of the tax collector? ("O God, be merciful to me a sinner.")
9. How can we welcome new students to our school and classroom?
10. If you were giving a party, what could you do to make sure everyone was having a good time?

Activities

1. Choose a story-telling partner and for two minutes each tell the other person about a time when someone made you feel welcome.
2. Outline your foot on a banner. Put your name on the footprint with something special about yourself. On the banner print the words: STEP RIGHT IN TO GRADE ____ AND MAKE YOURSELF AT HOME. Put your welcome banner up on your classroom door.
3. With 2 or 3 other students act out a story about being welcomed.
4. Choose a primary grade student to whom you can tell this parable. Then with the student illustrate the story. Display it on a school bulletin board.

JUNIOR HIGH LEVEL

1. Read LK 18:9-14. List the similarities and differences in the two stories.
2. Look up these stories and list the other things you discover about the professional religious in Jesus' time. LK 11:37-54; LK 12:1-4, 12 and LK 14:1-11.
3. The stories in Gal. 1:11-24 and JN 3:1-21 tell of other pharisees. How are these pharisees different from the others you have read about?
4. Look up these quotes and compare the other tax collectors in the Gospel of Luke: LK 5:27-32 and LK 19:1-10. What kind of people were they and how did Jesus relate to them?
5. What does it mean to be popular? (various answers)
6. How can being popular be used for the benefit of others and not just yourself? Or can it?
7. Which of the people in the parable acted most like Jesus? Why?
8. How can you welcome new students to your school or classroom?

9. At the end of the Luke story (LK 18:14), the Gospel writer explains how a person shall be exalted. How is this different from what society and our own peer group believes?

Activities
1. Imagine you are giving the party of the century. Make out a guest list of 10 special people in the world you would invite along with your other friends. Then with one other person plan 5 specific ways in which you can make everyone feel welcome.
2. You are on trial for being the most popular person in your class. Write a defense for the jury that explains all the good that can come from being popular.
3. Divide the class into two teams and debate this question: Popularity is only based on external appearances.
4. Choose one of the following proverbs and with a discussion partner explain how it is related to the parable. Prv 26:1; Prv 22:9; Prv 22:2.
5. Draw a spider's web. At each intersection, put the names of the characters in the story. Describe in a paragraph how the connections between the characters make the story and web's design more interesting.

   Note: The origin of the Pharisees can be traced back to the Maccabean Revolt. They were strong supporters of the Torah. They were not priests but lay scholars and teachers. In 90 A.D. they determined the contents of the Hebrew Bible.

CHAPTER VIII

The One Thank You

(Luke 17:11-19)

In the ten leper story, Jesus is described by the Gospel writer as journeying to Jerusalem. On his way he meets ten lepers in a village. They know Jesus and call out to him for mercy, not for curing. Jesus does not cure them there, but sends them to the priests who are the ones who can certify them as being able to rejoin the community.

All ten leave and on the way they are all cured. One, a Samaritan, realizing that he is cured goes back to give thanks. The other nine do not return. They are anxious to be certified as clean and to enter into the community life once again.

When Jesus is confronted by the one thankful leper who is a foreigner, he asks where are the other nine. The leper does not answer, but is acknowledged by Jesus as a person whose gratitude and faith have brought him health and wholeness. This health and wholeness are more than just physical. They have brought him salvation. Salvation from his alienated way of life as a leper and salvation for new life back into relationship with the community. His own sickness has been healed and now he is freed to be concerned with others. He has moved from the pain of a private world to the wider world of compassion and love.

Reflection Questions
1. As a teacher how do I show my students that I am a thankful person?
2. How do I show the parents, other teachers, and those in authority that I am grateful for their support?
3. When parents don't seem supportive, how can I provide them with opportunities to be involved with their children?

THE ONE THANK YOU

The _____ (name of school) baseball team had a great coach _____ (name of student). She/he worked hard with the nine team members and the relief pitcher, _____. They had lost every game the year before, but now the new coach had made them feel like winners.

She/he spent extra time with _____ (name of relief pitcher) who was a year younger than everyone else and not accepted by the others.

All during spring practice, coach _____ (name) encouraged them and after their last practice, she/he treated them to _____ (a kind of food) at _____ (local food place).

All during the season coach _____ (name) helped them. They won every game and were in the championship.

In the ninth inning with the bases loaded and two outs, _____, the relief pitcher, was called into the game. There were three balls and two strikes on the hitter from _____ (name of rival school). Coach _____ came out to the mound and said to _____ (relief pitcher),

"You can do it." Then with everyone holding their breath, _____ (relief pitcher) threw the ball and the umpire called out:

"Strike three." They won the championship. The whole team ran on to the field yelling: "We're number one."

As all 10 players left the locker room chanting, _____, the relief pitcher, ran back to the coach and said:

"Thanks for everything you did for me and the team."

The coach looked at _____ and said:

"Weren't there ten players on the team? Where are the other nine?"

PRIMARY LEVEL
1. How many games had the team won the year before? (none)
2. How did the new coach help them? (she/he made them feel like winners, she/he spent time with them, she/he took them for a treat)
3. Why wasn't the relief pitcher accepted? (he was a year younger)
4. What happened in the championship game? (they won because of the pitcher)
5. Who was the only one who thanked the coach? (the relief pitcher)
6. In the story who should we most be like? Why? (the pitcher, the coach)
7. Why do you think that the other nine did not thank the coach? (accept any reasonable answer)
8. Why did the pitcher thank the coach? (accept any reasonable answer)
9. Think of a time when you did not say thank you and you should have. Tell about that time.
10. Think of different ways to say thank you. (by being nice, giving a gift, a flower, a note)

11. Think of a person that always says thank you.
    Describe what this person is like.

Activities
1. Choose a play-acting partner. Pantomime a thank
   you story and have the class guess what is going on.
2. Make a list of people in the school that the class
   should thank. Vote on the one person that you
   should thank the most. Make a Thank You banner
   ("You Deserve a Hand") and as a way of signing it
   use a stamp pad for each student to make their
   fingerprints.
3. Read the original parable of the ten lepers and list all
   the ways it is like the modern story.
      Note: If baseball is not a popular game for your
   students then adapt the parable to fit kickball, dodge-
   ball, or any other game.

INTERMEDIATE LEVEL
1. How did the new coach help the team? (treating them
   like winners, spending more time with each player)
2. Why didn't the team accept the relief pitcher? (he was
   a year younger)
3. How did they win the championship game? (the relief
   pitcher struck the last person out)
4. Who thanked the coach? (only the relief pitcher)
5. How did the coach respond to the relief pitcher?
   (Where are the other nine?)
6. Give some examples of the times when you say thank
   you.
7. In your opinion, why is it important to show thankfulness? (accept any reasonable answer)
8. What are other ways to say thank you? (write a note,
   flowers, gift)
9. How can we show our parents that we are grateful?
   (accept any reasonable answer)

10. In your opinion, should the coach ever help the other nine again?

Activities
1. Read the original Ten Lepers parable (LK 17:11-19) and in groups of 3 or 4, list how the two stories are the same and different.
2. Invent your own story with the same moral and act it out in a skit with others in your class.
3. Make a "Thank You for Listening" card. Then go to a younger class and choose a student to whom you can retell the parable. Then give the listener the "thank you" card.

JUNIOR HIGH LEVEL
1. Read LK 17:11-19 and list the similarities and the differences between the two stories.
2. Why were the leper that gave thanks and the relief pitcher considered outsiders? (the leper was a foreigner, the pitcher was a year younger)
3. If nine came back to give thanks and the outsider didn't, how would that change the effect of the story? Would that be the kind of story Jesus would tell? Why or why not? (it would not have the same impact since the outsider was already being condemned. Probably, Jesus would not tell a story like that because his stories lead the listener to different thinking, which is based on surprise.)
4. In what ways can people be outsiders? (accept any reasonable answer)
5. How do we feel when the outsider is praised or successful? Why?
6. Take a stand for or against this statement: Thankfulness must be a part of friendship.
7. List the people to whom you are most grateful and why. In what ways can we say thank you to those people? (note, gift, flowers, courtesy)

8. The word Eucharist means thanksgiving. Why is the Eucharist a thanksgiving celebration? (we are thankful for Jesus in our lives and for the family of believers to whom we are united by our baptism.

Activities
1. With one other person and using the Book of Psalms select a Psalm of Thanksgiving and illustrate it. Present it to the class explaining: Why is the psalmist grateful? What are the other feelings in the psalm? Why did you choose it?
2. In a group of 3 or 4, act out a skit in which an outsider is the hero.
3. Research why the Samaritans and the people from Galilee where considered outsiders. Are there other groups like that today? Do minority groups fit in this category? Why or why not?
4. As a class create your own:

   a) litany of thanksgiving; and,

   b) examination of conscience using the failure to say "Thank You" as a basis for your litany of sorrow.

   Use them in a prayer or penance service or Eucharistic Celebration.

CHAPTER IX

The Sorry Story

(Luke 7:36-47)

Again the Gospel writer uses the context of sharing a meal as the setting for the penitent woman. While Jesus is having dinner at the house of a pharisee, a woman with the reputation of a sinner comes to him. Her tears of sorrow wash Jesus' feet. She wipes them with her hair and perfumes them with oil. In answer to Simon's judgmental thoughts which question Jesus as a prophet, Jesus tells a story about two debtors. One owes a small amount and the other a large amount. On questioning Simon as to which of the two would be most grateful when the debt is cancelled, the Pharisee answers logically. Naturally, it would be the one whose debt is larger.

Jesus' affirmation of Simon's correct response becomes an accusation of truth directed at Simon's small heartedness. No water was provided for Jesus' feet so that he could clean them from the dusty roads. No kiss of welcome or oil for anointing his head was given to the guest. Simon's lack of hospitality personifies the

smallness of his love. He is concerned not about relationship, but external appearances.

Simon not only doubts that Jesus is a prophet, but
his pride hardens his heart against others who are not
righteous according to the law. Jesus confronts Simon's
self-righteous indignation with the new law of unconditional love that relates repentance and forgiveness
with faith and salvation (verses 48-50).

As teachers we often find ourselves in the place of
the professional religious. The initial feeling of vocation
had been an intimately personal religious experience, a
conversion- surprise responded to with an open heart.
It began as process, but then became stuck in sameness
and certainty. As a result, the gift of being called turns
into a "separating from" others instead of a "reaching
out" to others. This division often happens in our own
ministry and provides a continuing cycle of alienation
instead of forgiveness and reconciliation.

Vocation can easily be used as an excuse to feel that
we have the answers for others. This is different from
Jesus' question-asking strategy. He doesn't give answers. Instead he provides contextually relevant stories
that liberate, challenge, and empower the listeners to
decide for themselves. Jesus' stories lure the listeners
to dig deeply into their own lives and to trust and value
their own experiences.

Reflection Questions
1. What do I do to become sensitive to the other
   teachers/catechists who minister in the local community of faith?
2. How do I share my own faith experience with those
   who are community with me?
3. In what practical ways do I encourage the faith
   community to celebrate the hospitality of Jesus?

THE SORRY STORY

Once upon a time there was a certain religious person _____, (name of student) and he/she invited Jesus to have dinner with him/her. A man/woman/teenager who was a _____ (drug addict, alcoholic, homeless person, derelict) from the local soup kitchen in _____ (name of a poor area) heard where Jesus was visiting. As they were sitting down to eat _____ (name of student) forced his/her way in, threw him/herself at Jesus' feet and cried.

Wiping Jesus' feet with his/her (sleeve/skirt), he/she gave him a _____ (name of flower) that he/she had picked on his/her way in. When _____ (name of religious person) saw this he said to him/herself,

"This person is ruining my dinner party. He/she is such a troublemaker. He/she is always doing wrong things."

Jesus said to him/her: "_____ (name), listen carefully. Two people owed money. One owed $5,000 and the other owed $500. Since neither one could pay both debts were erased. Which of the two was more grateful?"

_____ said: "The one that owed the most."

Jesus then looked at the person and said: "_____ (name of person) came in and welcomed me with tears of gladness and brought me a flower as a sign of his/her love. You did not even greet me at the door. That is why the wrong things he/she has done are forgiven because he/she has loved much."

Note: Jesus could be replaced with name of local bishop, school principal, parish pastor, or minister.

PRIMARY LEVEL

1. With whom was Jesus having dinner? (varies according to choice)
2. Why did the religious person become upset when the uninvited person came in? (he/she thought he/she was ruining his/her party)
3. What did the person do to show Jesus he/she was happy to see him? (he/she brought him a flower)
4. How could Jesus tell he/she was sorry for the things he/she had done? (he/she was crying)
5. What story did Jesus tell the religious person? (about the two people who owed money, both were forgiven)
6. Which of the two people who owed money was the happiest? (the one who owed the most)
7. Think about a time when you did something wrong. How did you feel when the person forgave you?
8. Which person showed that they loved Jesus the most, the religious person or the uninvited person? Why?
9. How can you show people that you love them? Parents? Friends? Neighbors? (accept any reasonable answer)

Activities

1. Being sorry is like glue. It fixes things up. Choose a partner to act out a "glue" story. Have the class guess what is happening.
2. Make a happy heart with two sides. Write your first name on one half and your last name on the other. Use them in your next "sorry" prayer service. Start out with one half of the broken heart pinned on each child. Hold hands and say the Our Father, then give each other the sign of peace. After the service take both sides and put them on your "Happy" bulletin board.

3. As a class make a list of the things for which you are sorry. Include this list in your prayer service or penitential rite at the next Eucharistic celebration.

INTERMEDIATE LEVEL
1. Retell the story in your own words.
2. Describe what kind of person came to the party uninvited.
3. Why did the religious person become upset when the person came in? (he/she was ruining his/her party)
4. How did the person show that he/she was happy to see Jesus? (he/she gave him a flower)
5. How did the person show that he/she was sorry for his/her wrongdoing? (the person cried)
6. Which of the two people who owed money was the most grateful? (the one that was forgiven the most)
7. Why did Jesus tell the story about the two people who owed money? (he wanted to show that no sin is too bad to be forgiven)
8. Think about a time when you were forgiven. How did you feel?
9. In the Our Father, what does it mean to "forgive us as we forgive those who trespass against us?"
10. Read LK 7:36-47 and discuss how the two stories are similar and how they differ.

Activities
1. Pretend you are a newspaper reporter and you are interviewing guests at the dinner party. With three other students present the interviews as part of the nightly newscast.
2. In groups of 2 or 3 list all the ways you can welcome someone. Then act one of those ways.
3. Imagine you are a storyteller on another planet in the year 2234. Invent your own story that will express the same idea, but change the characters.

4. Divide your class into two teams and defend your opinion about this statement: It is easy to forgive, but hard to forget.

JUNIOR HIGH LEVEL

1. Read LK 7:36-47. Compare and contrast (find the similarities and differences) between the two stories.
2. How did the person show that he/she was sorry for his/her wrongdoing? (tears, flower, and the fact that he/she came uninvited to the party)
3. What was the attitude of the host? Did he have a right to be upset? (he/she was embarrassed and upset, point out that he/she was judging the person's moral character)
4. How do we judge others? (usually by external appearances)
5. Will Rogers, the American humorist, once said: "I never met a person I didn't like." In your opinion how could anyone honestly say this?
6. What does Jesus mean when he says: "The wrong things he/she has done are forgiven because he/she has loved much."
7. Unconditional love means accepting a person no matter what they do. That's how Jesus loves us. In your opinion how can we do the same, or can we? Have there been other people in history who have achieved this? Parents? Friends?
8. In the short story "Cask of the Amontillado," Edgar Allan Poe writes an amazing story about revenge. Discuss how forgiveness and revenge are related.

Activities

1. Pretend you are a talk show host and with three other students (playing Jesus, the host, and the person) put on a TV show. Interview them about their

personal lives as well as the incident at the dinner party.

2. Choose one of these proverbs: Prv 13:7, Prv 12:16, Prv 14:21. In a small group discuss how it relates to the parable. Summarize your ideas and prepare a presentation for the class. Or write a story or skit that illustrates the proverb of your choice.

3. As a class make a list of all the ways in which we judge others. Use this as a penitential rite in a Eucharistic celebration, penance, or prayer service.

4. With another person use this parable and create three new commands that Jesus would give to his followers in the next century. Support your choice of "rules" with an explanation.

5. Guided imagery: Imagine a time when you were angry or disappointed with yourself. What did you learn from that situation? How did it help you grow? Now imagine yourself forgiving yourself. How does this self-forgiveness make you feel?

CHAPTER X

The Busy Teacher

(Luke 18:1-8)

In the original parable, the main character is the widow who demands her rights from a corrupt judge. After being worn out from the widow's perserverance, the judge finally does act justly. In the Jewish social laws of Exodus 22:21-24, the powerless widow is held in great respect and her cry has "power" to move God. Luke clearly expresses this vision of God acting on the behalf of the oppressed. For the Gospel writer God is not an unmoved, detached, philosophical principal, but one who cares and is involved with the actual world. It is a hopeful vision for a world fragmented by social and political chaos in the first century and in this century.

The Christian community, during Luke's time, was definitely a powerless minority facing the power of the dominant society. It was this struggle for identity in the midst of persecution that shaped Luke's understanding of how God acts within the history of the believing community. The Lucan Gospel is a testimony to Jesus' mission of proclaiming "liberty to captives," "sight to the blind," and "a year of favor from the Lord" (LK 4:18-19).

This mission is one that Luke knows the early Christians must carry out themselves. To fight injustice with an abuse of power or silence cannot be consistent with what it means to be a Christian.

In the everyday business of living, it seems that the busy-ness of ministry takes the place of care-fulness. This care-fulness should be for ourselves as well as for others. How many times has the challenge of ministry become a burden instead of a joy? The familiar adage that we cannot give what we do not have is a truism that has serious implications for each of us. If we cannot be happy as we serve others, then we should not serve. Our needs are just as important as the needs of those we serve. To judge ourselves relentlessly is to make it easier for ourselves to judge others just as harshly. To accept ourselves with both our talents and weaknesses is to empower ourselves to accept others more easily.

Jesus' message of unconditional love reveals the kind of God who is involved, moment by moment, in our lives. Jesus God is the God of the covenant relationship, of *hesed* or steadfast love. It is a God who cares and interacts with the world. God as ruthless moralist is replaced by God as compassionate lover. This exemplifies how we should look at our own ministry. To pay attention to the needs of ourselves and others is the care-filled message of a God who participates in our life and is touched by our experiences.

Reflection Questions
1. How do I respond to the questions, doubts, needs, and problems of my students, my friends, my family? How can I empower others to value their own experiences and discover their own answers?

2. How do I find opportunities to praise each student? How do I encourage students to praise and interact with each other?
3. How do I listen to and acknowledge my own needs as important? Am I gentle with myself or am I demanding and relentless in what I expect of myself and others?

THE BUSY TEACHER

Jesus told his listeners this story to show that we should pray always and never get discouraged.

Once in _____ (name of city) at _____ (name of school) there was a very busy teacher named _____ (name of student). The teacher always scolded her/his students for bothering her/him during class and had little time after school to stay and help them with their work.

She/he always told them: "You're old enough to settle your own problems. Don't come to me."

When the recess bell rang _____ (name of a student) would go out to play with the other students. Since he/she was smaller than the other children in his class, he/she was picked on by _____ (name of student), the class bully.

Every day _____ (name of small student) would come in from recess and say:

"_____, (name of teacher) today at recess _____ (name of bully) was making fun of me (gossiping about me, calling me names, won't let me play)." The teacher would always answer the same way:

"Can't you see that I am busy. You have to learn to solve your own problems."

Every day for a week, _____ (small student) said the same thing after each recess, and _____ (the teacher) answered with exactly the same words.

Finally, _____ (teacher) said to her/himself: "This student is wearing me out. Even though I am very busy and believe that students should work out their own problems, I have to settle this."

Then Jesus said: If the busy teacher finally listened to the student who would not give up, how much more will God answer those who ask for help.

Note: In this story, catechist can be substituted for teacher. Perhaps with a little more adjusting parent can be substituted. This would be more effective with Junior High students.

PRIMARY LEVEL
1. Why didn't the teacher (catechist, parent) help the child? (she/he was too busy, wanted children to solve their own problems)
2. What was the student's problem? (he/she was being picked on)
3. How long did the student ask the teacher for help? (every day for a week)
4. Did the teacher finally help? Why? (Yes, because the child was wearing her/him out)
5. Why did Jesus tell this story? (so people would not stop asking for help if they needed it)
6. Give an example of a time when you asked for help.
7. How did you feel when you were helped?
8. Who are the people in your life that you ask to help you? How can they help you?

Activity
1. Think about the person in your life that helps you most. Draw a Thank-you flower and on each petal write how that person has helped you. Give it to him/her.
2. Each student list three things that would make your school a happier place. Choose the one you want and

write an asking prayer to Jesus. Take it home to your parents and pray it tonight.
3. Think about some of the things your parents ask you to do. Which one do they ask most often? Draw a picture of yourself doing it the first time they ask. Give it to them as a promise of help.
4. With your acting partner pretend you are one of these community helpers and act out a skit: police officer, fire fighter, school secretary, and principal.

INTERMEDIATE LEVEL
1. Why didn't the teacher help the student? (she/he was too busy, wanted students to solve their own problems)
2. What was the student's problem? (he/she was being picked on)
3. Why did the teacher finally help the student? (the student had asked every day for a week)
4. Read LK 18:1-8. List the things that are different and the same. Why did Jesus tell this story? (to help us never get discouraged in prayer)
5. Who are some of the people you ask for help? How do they help you?
6. Who is the person in your life that helps you most? How and Why?
7. How do you feel when you are helped? How can you show that to the person who is helping you?
8. What 3 things would you pray for to make the world a happier place? Why?

Activities
1. Choose a storytelling partner and tell each other about a time when you asked for help and received it. After hearing each other's story decide which one you want to act out for the class.
2. Outline one of your hands and write a promise of help to someone. Give the helping hand to that person.

3. Find out the names of some of the helping organizations in your parish or community. Then ask one of
   its members to speak to your class about the services
   that they provide. Or interview them about their
   work. Then act out the interview for your class.
4. Draw a heart. Put your name on the front and write
   a prayer of petition for your family on the back.

JUNIOR HIGH LEVEL
1. Summarize the main points of the story. Then read
   LK 18:1-8 and list the similarities and the differences.
2. Did the teacher have a good reason for not solving
   the student's problem? Support your opinion with
   examples from your own experience.
3. Identify and then rank the three most important
   concerns in the world. Compose a prayer of petition
   about your number one concern.
4. Visualize how the world would be different if your
   prayer became a reality. Describe your new world in
   a paragraph. How can you help make this new world
   come true?
5. Read James 3:1-5 and explain why teachers will be
   called to strict responsibility. (the power of the word
   to influence)
6. Read James 2:14-17. In your opinion how does this
   excerpt from James relate to the parable? (faith and
   good works are connected so that prayer or petition
   and Christian service or action necessarily work
   together.)

Activities
1. Decide who the people are in your life that help you
   solve problems. Why and how do they help you?
   Which person helps you the most? Then choose a
   discussion partner with whom you can share your
   feelings.

2. As a class decide which one world concern is the most important to you. Decide which three people could help this situation. Compose a letter to the person who could help the most and send it.
3. In a group of three or four and using the Book of Psalms choose a psalm which is a prayer of petition. Explain what the psalm is asking for and why. In the class presentation, read it as a choral reading or take turns in the group reading by stanza.
4. Find modern songs that speak about personal or world problems. Bring them to class, play them, and discuss if the song is proposing a solution or is helping you discover an answer within yourself.

CHAPTER XI

An Anywhere, Anytime Parable

This story is a part of the fabric of my own personal life and that of my family's. It is one of my father's Depression stories. This one story, more than anything I was ever taught in a formal context, convinced me about the power of faith. It has been a "truth-experience" inherited from my family's past, and it continues to be the influential ethical norm that shapes my personal life.

My father was the little boy who invited the stranger to dinner. In East Los Angeles during the 1930s the phrase "mi casa es su casa" (My home is your home) had far reaching implications, especially if you were the oldest of eleven children. The empty place at my grandparent's table has become a poignantly powerful symbol of what Jesus was all about: "Welcome the stranger."

In the Rule of St. Benedict the axiom that shaped the rise of western monasticism was the exhortation to receive each guest as Christ himself. Today we see this mirrored in the ministry of Dorothy Day's Catholic Worker communities, Catherine Dougherty's Madonna Houses, Mitch Snyder's work in Washington, D.C., Mother Teresa's communities of men and women working with the poorest of the poor all over the world. The social dimension of the Gospel message is embodied in the fullness of sharing a meal, or whatever we have and are, with each other in a way that reconciles.

This unifying message is manifested in organizations of people who work for others in society who are estranged: the AIDS patients, the hungry, the powerless, the undocumented, the marginalized, those in our own families, Churches, and neighborhoods with whom we do not agree. A world in pieces is not a world at all. It is this challenge of integration, of "welcoming home," that is the creative activity of the many being mutually enriched by each other. If we are not afraid or defensive about our "truth," then pluralism has the potential for a kind of wealth that leads to health and wholeness.

The influence of the many does not of necessity lead to chaos. Rather, as emphasized by the stories in this anthology, the novel provides an opportunity for feeling and thinking about our own worldview in a new way. Jesus captured the imagination of his listeners by "surprising" them with the unexpected. He turned their accepted worldview upside down and challenged them to reflection and action. He used the social, cultural, and ethnic issues of his time to help them discover the "truth- experiences" within themselves. Then, he left them with a choice. This is the creative activity of the Gospel message that engages us.

We are influenced by our own past tradition, religiously, culturally, and personally. By accepting both the richness and limitations of this past, we anticipate a future that is present in every moment of our own ministry. This bringing together of past and future in the present IS the creative activity of the Gospel message. It is forever new because its universality transcends a specific time and place by relating to every particular time and place.

In the final analysis, this is the purpose for which I have written these stories. The eleven patterns for storytelling provide a way to continue this creative process by making the Gospel ever new. It is a way of weaving together youthful dreams so that the fabric that emerges is lovely, not because of the sameness, but because of the contrasting diversity. The Gospel becomes the patterned fabric for a global design.

AN ANYWHERE, ANYTIME PARABLE

The times were hard in _____ (city) on _____ (street) and the _____ (name) family had _____ (number) children to feed. The house was near the _____ (train, bus or etc.)and every day when the (train, bus or etc.) came in at _____ (time), more homeless people came into the city looking for jobs. But there were no jobs because times were hard.

Every day people would walk by the _____ (family name) house and even though times were hard, the family always had an empty space at the table for anyone who would come to the door. Every morning they had _____ (type of food) for breakfast and every evening they had _____ (type of food) for dinner because that's all they could afford. But they had lots of it and there was always extra for anyone who stopped in.

The _____ (youngest, oldest child) walked to school every day and passed a _____ (soup kitchen, bread line) where people waited in line for food. This made him/her very sad because he/she knew that times were hard. One day he/she walked by a parked _____ (year, type of car) and saw someone sleeping inside it because she/he had no place to go. He/she passed by it every day for a week and each time he/she became sadder because times were hard.

Then the weather changed _____ (colder, hotter) because it was the month of _____ (name of month).

_____ (name of child) came home from _____ school and told his/her parent(s):

"Every day I pass a car with someone sleeping in it. They have no place to go and they're poor."

So the _____ (father, mother) said:

"Let's go invite them to dinner because times are hard."

So _____ (name of child) and his _____ (mother, father etc.) went to the car and said: "Come home to dinner with us. Times are hard."

So the person came home and was welcomed as part of the family. She/he stayed for two years and was called _____ (auntie, uncle, etc.)

PRIMARY LEVEL
1. Did the child come from a big family? (yes)
2. Where was the child's home? (near the bus/train station)
3. How did the family share? (they left an empty place at the table for every meal)
4. What did they have every morning and evening? Why? (whatever choice was made and because it was cheap)
5. Where did the child see someone sleeping? (in a car)
6. When the child told his/her parents, what did they decide to do? (invite her/him to dinner)

7. Why did they eat the same thing every day? (they were poor)
8. Why did the person feel welcomed? (she/he was invited to dinner and treated like one of the family)
9. How do you know she/he became part of the family? (she/he stayed for two years and was called auntie/uncle)
10. How was the child acting like Jesus? (he/she wanted to share what he/she had)
11. How can we help those who are hungry at school? (we can share)

Activities
1. Arrange a box lunch social so that each student brings a lunch for someone else, then draw names.
2. Together as a class write on the chalkboard a special lunch blessing and recite it together.
3. Draw a picture of your favorite food on your dining room table. Then draw people that you would like to invite for dinner around the table.

INTERMEDIATE LEVEL
1. How do you know that times were hard? (bread lines, homeless people)
2. Why did the child decide to tell his/her parents about the homeless person? (the weather was changing).
3. Who invited the homeless person to dinner? (the parents)
4. How did the family make her/him feel welcome? (they shared their dinner)
5. Why was the end of the story surprising? (because she/he stayed for two years and was called auntie/uncle)
6. What does it mean to make someone welcome? (to make them feel like they belong)

7. How can we make people feel welcome at school, at home, and in our neighborhood? (accept any reasonable answer)

Activities
1. With a think-partner, read MT 25:34-40 and list all the ways we can serve Jesus. Then choose one way and make a skit out of it to perform for the class. Invite others in the class to participate.
2. Choose a scripture partner and Read MT 22:34-39. What are the two great commandments and how does this parable show them both?
3. Arrange a box lunch social. Choose names and prepare a special blessing for your chosen person.

JUNIOR HIGH LEVEL
1. How can you tell that times were hard? (soup lines, homeless people, poor food)
2. What made the child decide to tell his/her parents about the person in the car? (the weather was changing)
3. How do you know that the homeless person was welcomed? (she/he stayed for two years and was called auntie/uncle)
4. What is hospitality? (to make someone feel at home)
5. What hospitality did the family show to the homeless person? (they shared their food)
6. Even though the family was poor why did they share their food? (accept any reasonable answer)
7. What kind of hospitality can we show at school, at home, and in our neighborhood? (accept any reasonable answer)
8. Why is it sometimes difficult to show hospitality? (accept any reasonable answer, emphasize that it is often difficult to accept people who are different from us)

Activities
1. Read *Dreams Deferred* by Langston Hughes and discuss in groups of 2 or 3 how the poem relates to the parable.
2. Find out about Dorothy Day and the Catholic Worker Movement. How does this organization help the poor? Instead of a written report, work with a group to write a play about any event in Dorothy Day's life or in the life of the community. If there is a Catholic Worker community in your city, invite one of the members to come to speak about their work.
3. With a research team, find out which organizations in your city feed the poor. Present your findings to the class and decide on one specific thing your class could do to help.
4. With a think-partner, read Isaiah 55:1-13. Discuss what kind of food the prophet is talking about. How does it relate to the parable? (the food in Isaiah is God's own life of love, the family shared this life of love by sharing their home)

RESOURCES

There are certain theological, philosophical, and psychological assumptions that have influenced my ministry in religious education. These assumptions have arisen from my family background, from my own life experiences, and from books that have influenced my development as a practical theologian. In the context of our own particular ministry, the challenge for each of us is to continue expanding our horizons so that we grow not just in one way, but in many ways. The following bibliography is a small sample of some of the significant writings that have shaped my perceptions about the issues involved in religious education within a pluralistic society.

Andrews, Lynn V. *Medicine Woman.* San Francisco: Harper and Row, Publishers, 1981. A fascinating autobiographical tale of religious experience and education under the apprenticeship of a Cree medicine woman. Her sequels are *Flight of the Seventh Moon* (1984), *Jaguar Woman* (1985), *Star Woman (1986), and Crystal Woman (1987).*

Belenky, M.F., *et al. Women's Ways of Knowing: The Development of Voice, Self, and Mind.* New York: Basic, 1986. A necessary complement to Kohlberg's work.

Bellah, Robert N., *et al. Habits of the Heart.* Berkeley, CA.: University of California Press, 1985. A fascinating study about individualism and the conflicts in values in contemporary American society.

Berger, Peter. *The Heretical Imperative.* New York: Anchor Press, 1979. An excellent source for getting in touch with the dilemmas of modernity.

Brueggemann, Walter. *The Creative Word.* Philadelphia: Fortress Press, 1982. Shows the relationship between the canon of the Old Testament and educational ministry.

The Prophetic Imagination. New York: Fortress Press, 1978. Exciting presentation of the prophetic role in ministry.

Chardin, Pierre Teilhard de. *The Divine Milieu.* New York: Harper and Row, 1968. Chardin's vision of the cosmos is hypnotic and profound.

Birch, Charles and John B. Cobb, Jr. *The Liberation of Life.* Cambridge: Cambridge University Press, 1984. A stimulating investigation of all kinds of life in the biotic community and the ecological-ethical implications for people of faith.

Cobb, John B. *Beyond Dialogue.* Philadelphia: Fortress Press, 1982. Valuable discussion about the mutual transformation of the religious traditions of Christianity and Buddhism.

Christ in a Pluralistic Age. Philadelphia: The Westminster Press, 1975. A challenging and refreshing approach to Christology.

God and the World. Philadelphia: The Westminster Press, 1969. An insightful, coherent investigation of the doctrine of God and its implications in forming our approach to the world.

Cox, Harvey. *Religion in the Secular City.* New York: A Touchstone Book, 1984. A creative and prophetic exploration of grassroots religion in today's secular world.

Eckhart, Meister. *Breakthrough.* Introduction and commentaries by Matthew Fox, OP. New York: Image Books, 1980. This new

translation of the work of the 14th century Dominican describes a creation-centered spirituality, which is prodoundly
relevant to our own time.

Erikson, Erik H. *Life History and the Historical Moment.* New
York: W. W. Norton and Company, Inc., 1975. Erikson's contribution to understanding identity formation is one important
voice in the theory of developmental psychology.

Fowler, James W. *Stages of Faith.* New York: Harper and Row,
1981. A valuable work on the psychology of human development, but should be balanced with a more non-linear approach
as in late Piaget's structuralism, Maria Harris' work, and
Whitehead's *Aims of Education.*

Foster, Charles R. *Teaching in the Community of Faith.* Nashville:
Abingdon Press, 1982. An important work with a particular
sensitivity to our multi-cultured society.

Freud, Sigmund. *The Future of an Illusion.* New York: W. W.
Norton and Company, Inc., 1961. If you haven't read much of
Freud, this is a good way to begin. There are some fascinating
ideas to play around with in this small book.

Gilligan, Carol. *In a Differnt Voice.* Cambridge, Mass: Harvard
University Press, 1982. An interesting and insightful book on
the psychology of woman's development.

Groome, Thomas H. *Christian Religious Education.* New York:
Harper and Row, 1980. Groome covers a wide range of questions and provides his praxis approach as a methodology.

Hall, Edward T. *The Silent Language.* New York: Anchor Books,
1973. An anthropologist's view of the elements of culture and
how they inform our ways of communication.

James, William. *The Varieties of Religious Experience.* New York:
Penguin Books, 1983. A classic study of the psychology of
religion that provides a healthy approach to religious pluralism.

Jung, Carl G. *Psychology and Religion.* London and New Haven:
Yale University Press, 1938. Jung discusses the richness of
religious symbolism from a variety of sources.

Knitter, Paul. *No Other Name?* New York: Orbis Books, 1985. A good sourcebook for investigating the Christian attitudes toward world religions.

Lifton, Robert Jay. *The Life of the Self.* New York: A Touchstone Book, 1976. A tremendously helpful resource in understanding the psychology of the "self."

Macquarrie, John. *Principles of Christian Theology.* New York: Charles Scribner's Sons, 1977. A necessary sourcebook for personal reflection on systematic theology.

Macy, Joanna. *Despair and Personal Power in the Nuclear Age.* Baltimore: New Society Publishers, 1983. An exciting book that opens up in practical ways the potential for human compassion.

McFague, Sallie. *Metaphorical Theology.* Philadelphia: Fortress Press, 1982. Creative, insightful exploration for models of God in religious language.

Merton, Thomas. *Zen and the Birds of Appetite.* New York: New Directions Book, 1968. This is Merton at his best. It provides wonderful insights into an East-West dialogue.

Metz, Johannes B. *Theology of the World.* New York: The Seabury Pres, 1969. Intellectually stimulating approach to understanding the necessity of de-privatizing religion.

Moore, Mary Elizabeth. *Education for Continuity and Change.* Nashville: Abingdon Press, 1983. Insightful investigation into understanding the development of tradition.

Niebuhr, Richard H. *The Responsible Self.* New York: Harper and Row, 1963. An essential book for investigating the role of the self in relation to society.

Nolan, Albert. *Jesus Before Christianity.* New York: Orbis Books, 1978. A wonderful book that presents deeper understanding of Jesus in *his* century.

O'Brien, David J. and Thomas A. Shannon. *Renewing the Earth.* New York: Image Books, 1977. Important collection of Catholic Documents on Peace, Justice, and Liberation.

Rahner, Karl. *Foundations of Catholic Faith.* New York: The Seabury Press, 1978. Some heavy going, but invaluable systematic approach to questions of faith.

Schaef, Anne Wilson. *Women's Reality.* San Francisco: Harper and Row, Publishers, 1985. An important book in helping men and women understand the psycho-social differnces in each other.

Co-Dependence, Misunderstood—Mistreated. San Francisco: Harper and Row, Publishers, 1986. An invaluable work that will help those in ministry understand the systemic nature of the addictive process in all our lives.

Sloyan, Gerard. *Jesus in Focus.* Mystic, Connecticut: Twenty-Third Publications, 1983. Excellent approach to Jesus in the biblical context.

Tillich, Paul. *The Courage To Be.* Mass: Yale University Press, 1952. Based on the Terry Lectures delivered at Yale, these chapters form a challenging reflection on the experience of life.

Turner, Victor. *The Ritual Process.* New York: Aldine Publishing Company, 1969. A fascinating study of ritual symbols and their meaning in African tribes. It provides a way for us to look at universal patterns of imaging life, death, and rebirth within the community context.

Westerhoff, John H. *Will Our Children Have Faith?* New York: The Seabury Press, 1983. This work contributes insights into the role of the community in the transmission of faith.

Whitehead, Alfred North. *Adventure of Ideas.* New York: The Free Press, 1961.

Aims of Education and Other Essays. New York: The Free Press, 1961. A wonderfully insightful and invaluable description of the cyclic rhythms in the process of education (Romance, Precision, and Generalization).

Modes of Thought. New York: The Free Press, 1966.

Religion in the Making. New York: The Macmillan Company, 1954. If you want a challenge and are interested in the ongoing questions of the "one" and the "many," permanence and

change, pick up Whitehead's works. There will be some difficult
reading, but tremendously worthwhile.

Conspicuously missing from the above bibliography are books dealing with three important interre-
lated areas of concern: wellness, spirituality, and
praxis-oriented resources. Here are just a few sugges-
tions.

Wellness

Gratton, Carolyn. *Trusting: Theory and Practice*. New York:
Crossroad Publishing Co., 1982.

Kelsey, Morton. *Caring: How Can We Love One Another*. New
York: Paulist Press, 1981.

MacNutt, Francis. *The Power to Heal*. Notre Dame, Indiana: Ave
Maria Press, 1983.

Periodicals

*Religious Education: The Journal of the Religious Education
Association and the Association of Professors and Researchers
in Religious Education*. 409 Prospect Street, New Haven,
Connecticut 06511-2177.

Catechist. 2451 East River Road, Dayton, Ohio 45439.

Spirituality

The most influential writers in my life have been
Meister Eckhart, John of the Cross, Teresa of Avila,
Thomas Merton, Charles de Foucauld, Hildegard of
Bingen, Mechtild of Magdeburg, and Mohandas K.
Gandhi, Benedict of Nursia.

The following writers have influenced my Native
American spirituality: Black Elk, Sun Bear, Evelyn
Eaton, Paula Gunn Allen, and Anne Cameron.